# SPECULATIVE FRE

A HISTORICAL

## LECTURE

UPON

## THE ORIGIN OF CRAFT AND HIGH GRADE FREEMASONRY,

AND

### SHOWING THE GREAT ANTIQUITY OF THE COMBINED SYSTEM,

*Delivered before the Brethren of the Palatine and Jerusalem Chapter, No. 2 on the Roll of the Sovereign Sanctuary of the Antient and Primitive Rite of Masonry in and for the United Kingdom of Great Britain and Ireland, in assembly at their place of meeting, the Grosvenor Hotel, Deansgate, Manchester, 31st March, 1883:*

### BY JOHN YARKER,

33°, 90°, 96°, F.S.Sc., &c., &c.,

FORMERLY OF THE LODGES INTEGRITY, MANCHESTER, AND FIDELITY, DUKINFIELD; PAST MASTER OF ALL DEGREES, AND HONORARY MEMBER OF MANY HOME AND FOREIGN BODIES; PAST SENIOR GRAND WARDEN OF THE GRAND LODGE, GREECE; PAST GRAND CONSTABLE OF THE TEMPLE IN ENGLAND; &c., &c.

---

PUBLISHED FOR THE PALATINE AND JERUSALEM CHAPTER BY BROTHER JOSEPH HAWKINS, 33°-95°, GRAND MASTER OF LIGHT FOR THE NORTHERN COUNTIES, ROBY, LIVERPOOL.

# SPECULATIVE

# FREEMASONRY

John Yarker

My Dear Brethren.—

The expert Mason cannot fail but look with regret upon the sad want of authentic knowledge which exists amongst Masonic brethren of all ranks and degrees : it is this deficiency which, in a great measure, leads to the schisms prevailing, and to that want of brotherly-love which we find so general in the rival systems. With greater knowledge, Masons would be more tolerant and more just to each other. It was in some measure to remedy this that the Antient and Primitive Rite was organised in this and other countries, and in holding out a fraternal hand to all other Rites it aimed at promoting good feeling amongst Masons of all degrees. Hitherto it has had to fight its way against the great and organised opposition of another less tolerant system of 33 degrees solely by its own merits, and only requires to be known to be fully appreciated by the Craft. The sole condition for reception among us is moral worth, probity, and honour. The one great obstacle to its rapid success is, therefore, the apathy and indifference to learning which is so prevalent amongst Craft Masons, who because they belong to a rich and influential society have no better wants. If you speak to the youngest Master Mason about our most learned of all Rites, he may very likely reply to you in the words of one of these : "Oh! you are not recognised! you cannot expect a society founded by King Solomon to acknowledge the Modern High Degrees." Why, my Brethren, if in Masonry there is one thing more certain than another it is that these so-called Higher Mysteries—which a Craft Grand Lodge has no knowledge of, and cannot therefore be requested to patronise by recognition—have a better and more authentic history than Craft Masonry.

In the brief exposition which I am about to give you I will endeavour to be as concise as possible and avoid all unnecessary matter, though I fear that will render me somewhat dry and tedious. I will indicate to you, first, the history of Operative Masonry, and deal tenderly with it; second, the descent of the High Grades, and show their immense antiquity; third, the cause of the amalgamation of the two systems and the period of its occurrence : constituting in effect the derivation and descent of Freemasonry as we now have it. Lastly, I will give you some information in regard to the origin of our own Rite, with other particulars in reference to it and to Freemasonry generally.

(1.) It is admitted, almost universally, by those very Masonic antiquaries who decry the High Grades, that Craft Masonry as a ceremonial system had no existence before the year 1722, and that it is practising certain Mysteries on the erroneous assumption that they are very ancient. I do not entirely hold with those good brethren who express this opinion, but I do assert that our existing Craft and High Grade Mysteries, as a matter of antiquity, must stand or fall together, and it is actually the superior Mysteries which have at various times during the last 5,000 years given off and organised numerous Craft Associations. By this term I indicate various operative brotherhoods, embracing workmen who laboured as masons, joiners, plasterers, slaters, smiths, and painters; for the Operative Guilds embraced members of these confederated trades. The comparatively recent comminatory action of the Papal Church is adduced as a proof that our present Solomonic Masonry had no existence until recent times. But it *is* provable that the old Masons had guilds and assemblies, with trade secrets protected by oaths, grips, and words, and that their somewhat symbolical ceremonies, although differing in detail amongst themselves, had much in common with each other and with existing trade unions. These workmen have such an organisation at this day, independently of our Freemasonry, which is a strong argument in favour of the views which have been put forward by those esteemed Masons who deny 200 years of antiquity to our Masonic Craft. These old guild ceremonies, without doubt, varied according to the High Grade Rite which constituted them, and, passing through unlearned hands, were badly preserved, for the scant nature of their ceremonies is proved by the well-preserved minutes of the old Operative Lodges of Scotland, extending far beyond 1717. The nature of the ancient Craft Ceremonies is clearly indicated in the ancient Craft Constitutions, and the old Minutes of the Scottish Operative Lodges—both of which series of documents show strict identity, and extend from the 16th to the 17th century. The ceremonial consisted in reading over certain rules applicable to the guidance of an ordinary stonemason's apprentice, upon which he was sworn to obey them, and received a grip and word. When he had faithfully served his seven years, he became a Fellow of Craft, or Journeyman Mason, was re-sworn and received a higher grip and word.

In apt illustration of the position which I intend to assume in my address to you this evening, I may inform you that the Masonic trade Yogams of the Hindus assert that their system was established in the morning of time by those very Rishis who constituted the high Yogams of the Brahmins and the Vedas. They are, in point of fact—as recently set forth in a protest to our Government, who claimed to give them a Chief Yoge—the ceremonies of a lower caste (namely, the Sudras, or Artizans), whilst the Brahmins have a high-caste system, analogous to the degrees of our Council. But the Sudra Yogams are able to hold their own, and assert that Visvakarman (or the Great Master Builder) is identical with the Vedaic Brahma, and that the symbolism of their architectural craft is convertible into the Nature Symbols of the order of Brahminical Theosophy. That this was so, also, in Egypt before the Christian era is proved by the recent discovery of Masonic Craft emblems at the base of Cleopatra's Needle, coupled with the symbology of the wonderful architecture of that mysterious land. It is, moreover, admitted by the learned that between ancient Egypt and India there was a convertibility or mutual recognition of Rites. In the European birthplace of Freemasonry we have very little—in reality, nothing tangible—to produce in the way of antiquity. But the great middle-age builders were the Society of Knights Templar, another high-grade secret system of the middle or warrior caste, preserved in the degrees of our Senate. It is not very improbable, on the face of what I shall advance to you, that these, in or about the 12th century, gave off the Craft organisation of the Operative Masonry claiming from Solomon's Temple.* This supposition is strengthened by the fact that the Templars, in A.D. 1118, acquired the site of Solomon's Temple, and that adjacent thereto existed a high-grade Rite of Mahommedan warriors who sought occult knowledge, with an organised system of seven secret degrees, afterwards increased to nine, under the prestige of King Solomon, of whose magical powers they have astonishing legends. I allude to the secret doctrine of the House of Wisdom, which originated the somewhat unenviable Society of Assassins, corresponding in its doctrines to the "Elu" degrees of the Ancient and Accepted Rite, which we have rejected as immoral and unworthy of our own.

At any rate, from this period there came down the stream of centuries such a society as Operative Freemasonry was before the year 1700; but its ceremonies, even in the same country, were not uniform. In France, these trade-unions

---

* Colonel W. J. B. Macleod Moore, of Laprarie, Canada, holds that the Benedictine monks had certain religious Mysteries of a symbolical nature, and that the Templars and Operative Masons derived these Mysteries from that source; and that each developed them to suit their own professions.

were often at actual war with the Masons of a different legend; and, near 1700, it was charged against some that the Candidate personated Christ. At the present day, the rivals over a legend are either the followers of the assassinated Master Jacques, Father Soubise, or Master Hiram; and these societies claim great antiquity, but give no proof of their legends. In Britain, we have no proof that Craft Masonry had either of these legends before 1723; but the probability is that it had the legend of the Hiram system in a much more meagre and unpolished form than now exists. In other words, the British Operative, or Craft Masons have left no record that they had an esoteric Mystery before the formation of the Grand Lodge at London. So much, for better or worse, is all that can be said for Craft Masonry; and I will now turn me round to those secret associations which, for want of a better word, I shall call High Grade Masons.

(II.) I shall proceed, with the intent of following their history, to inform you that, in all the most ancient nations— Chinese, Babylonian, Egyptian, Indian, Persian — there existed, and still exists, a certain secret School of Wisdom, which in all lands had certain degrees, with obligations of secresy, and ceremonial rites with tokens and words: they were either of seven or nine degrees, and the members, then and still, affiliate with distant Rites. Many modern Craft Freemasons have, like myself, become connected with the Oriental Societies. They have many points in common with the secret Cabala of the Jews, which probaby derives from the Schools of the Prophets, of which we find mention in the Jewish writings. They sought 10,000 years ago by arduous toil—and found it—the basis of religion, philosophy, and art: their faith was that of the proved religion, in which all the learned men of antiquity agreed. The first, after Moses, to publish their doctrine was the initiated Plato, often called the Divine Platon. A word to he that hath ears will be sufficient. The Egyptian "Book of the Dead," which in its primitive form is probably 10,000 years old, says: "As the sun died and rose again yesterday, so man dies and rises again." This (winter) sun was the (dying) son that was assassinated by the Great Serpent of the Heavens, Apophis. Its legend was the Mysterious Myth which the representative neophyte personated during his reception. The name and rites of this slain "Son of the Sun" varied amongst the nations as different languages do vary. In Chaldea it was Ghizdubar; in Egypt, Osiris; in Persia, Mythras; in India, Sita, or Kama; in Greece, Bacchus or Dionysos; in Germany, Baldur; in Syria, Adonis; in Samothrace,

Cadmillus; in Britain, Hu. Damascius and Suidas assert the identity of Osiris and Adonis; Clemens Alexandrinus, that of Dionysos and Atys; and Ausonius, that Bacchus, Osiris, Phanac, Dionysos, Liber, and Adonis were one and the same; while Macrobius informs us that Adonis, Atys, Osiris, Horus, and Liber were all equally the Sun. Damascius asserts that in one of the Temple manifestations of this divinity a mass of light appeared on the walls of the Temple: at first the fire-cloud appeared to be remote, but, advancing nearer, revealed a face divine and superhuman. In Operative Freemasonry of primitive times, the hero may have been Ur, or Urim—sun or light. In later Manichæism (a secret system of degrees) it was at times Mani; but with those who accepted the new faith, Jesus the Christ. In the Mohammedan associations it was and is Hakim, Ali, &c. In middle-age, Rosicrucianism, the Divine Jesus: as also with the Templars These legends are the same in essentials under whatever name the hero is known, and for the time the neophyte is the prototype. St. Augustine says (after he abandoned, or rather was refused, the esoteric degrees) that some Christian sects cursed all those who were supposed by implication to deny the actuality of Jesus by saying that "Zoroaster, Buddha, Jesus, Mani, and the Sun are one and the same;" and this statement is conclusive proof of that I have informed you. All things repeat themselves in cycles: for the Craft Mason of to-day curses the High Grades when refused admission, and, when we throw them open to all religions, we are accused of irreligion.

The old and learned Sages, or High Grade Masons, have left their history everywhere, and no student need be ignorant of it. The ancient Vedas expressly state that any member of the religious Mystery in the second or third degree who shall reveal the higher Mysteries before the prescribed time to members of the first or second degree shall be put to death and have his tongue cut out. Primitively, the first adepts were men profoundly versed in arts, science, and spiritual knowledge, who proceeded to enlarge their numbers by the admission of neophytes from neighbouring tribes. As their members increased, they emigrated far and wide, and established Colleges amongst all nations, which, on the model of the first, went on increasing their numbers. Originally celibates, some of them married and returned to the world, and had progeny, who founded the left-handed system, or sorcery. They were the "sons of God who took to themselves wives of the daughters of men."* This led to the next step,

---

* Vide " Book of Enoch."

in which the true Hierophants established difficult and dangerous proofs before the reception of a neophyte ; and the great Temple Mysteries of Egypt, upon which most of the others were modelled, were founded with all their secret and imposing receptions. Wars, and finally Christian intolerance, did the rest, and scattered the heirs of the Primitive Wisdom amongst all nations. There is a record at Rome which states that the Eleusenian Mysteries of Ceres and Dyonyses had been established in Britain. Various communities of monks and fraternities of knights continued the practice of the Mysteries, and even at this day the Madonna of Rome is an exact copy of the much more ancient Isis of Egypt.

The immediate successors of the Egyptian and Persian School of Wisdom were the Essenes and Manichees. At the period of the Crusades, Hakim's House of Wisdom ; the Cathari, the Templars, and their teachers the Sabeans of St. John ; the Gnostics, and the Cabalists of the Jews and Spanish Moors ; with other secret societies of like nature. The so-called Alchemists were of this school, and the middle-age Fire Philosophers.* That our present ceremonies are those of the ancients is proved by the paintings in Egyptian temples and tombs. That the ancient Mysteries had our Rose Croix ceremonies is proved by the language of the Sybils of the Temple, preserved in the Sybilline Oracles ; that they passed down to more modern times is indicated in the poetic language of the "Romance of the Rose," and in Dante, Chaucer, Gower, and the Troubadors ; and afterwards the same rites can be traced in the mystical writings of their successors, who have been termed Templars, Theosophists, Alchemists, Rosicrucians, and Gnostics, or "Knowing Ones"— a term well known to the Papal Church—not modern, as in the Egyptian "Book of the Dead," 5,000 years ago, an initiate is represented as saying to Osiris : "I am one of the 'Knowing Ones.'" Apulieus relates his reception into the Egyptian Mysteries in Greece, and his admission as a Pastophori in the College of Priests. His ceremonies closely resemble those still in use. And, moreover, he relates in symbolical fable how the Hierophant fed him upon a diet of *roses*, by which he was drawn from sensual nature and passions. Necessarily, in the course of ages, the ceremonials were changing, but the essential characteristics remained. In all time the Wisdom Society protected itself by a double or symbolical language, and there are many allusions in ancient writings to this fact. Dante expressly states that the

---

* Hargrave Jennings's "Rosicrucians" has much valuable information.

persecution of the Church had compelled him to change the style, and that therefore he sang in the hidden language of Platonic love: for, as the Church of Rome now bans Freemasonry, so in those days it banned and burned the western professors of our philosophy. They hid themselves from persecution in all costumes, threw themselves amongst the orders of monks and chivalry, and often wrote or sang themselves to the stake.* They were the life and soul of the secret Theosophical brotherhoods of the middle ages, and, as Fludd tells us, organised secret ceremonial Mysteries within the walls of the universities. Those who desire to understand the subject more fully will find the information in my unpretending work on "Speculative Freemasonry." These societies claimed to be, and actually were, the western successors of the ancient eastern Mysteries, and, though they were Christian professors, their faith was not that of Rome, for they expressly proclaimed the Pope as Antichrist, and that it was part of their duty to pull down his triple crown. These Rosicrucians of the 17th century—for such became the exoteric and generic name of the brotherhood in Europe—were justified in asserting their identity with the occult schools of India, which have for ages uninterruptedly practised their seven Mysteries as a Theurgic Rite.

Although there was a great similarity in ceremonies of the Wisdom Mysteries to those of modern Freemasonry (for the reason that the latter have been amended in modern times to imitate the House of Wisdom of seven stories), yet there was, and is, an essential difference between the two which I can only glance at here by saying that, whilst Freemasonry is only a symbol, the House of Wisdom is an actuality—ours is amusement, theirs, labour of the most severe description. The chief existing branches of to-day transmitted from ancient times are the African Mysteries; the Lebanon Druses and Ainsareeh; the Chinese Triad and the Japanese Celestial Brotherhood; the Hindu Temple Mysteries; and the Bektash, and other Dervish Sect Mysteries of Turkey, Persia, and Egypt. To these we may add certain western Freemasons; but it is somewhat dangerous to use the signs thereof, as "unknowing" members, or those who lack the Gnosis, have been assassinated for using the western signs wherewith to penetrate the Mysteries of the Eastern societies.† But the

* Read the works of Paracelsus, Behmen, Fludd, Vaughan, &c. Also Henry Morley's "Life of Cornelius Agrippa." The best single work on the subject is Gabriel Rosetti's "Disquisitions on the Anti-Papal Spirit which Produced the Reformation."

† A public reference to one case of this kind will be found recorded in the "Anacalypsis" of Brother Godfrey Higgins.

fact that our signs, secrets, symbols, and ceremonies have such a close resemblance to those of the Eastern mystic brotherhoods is the strongest proof you can have of the truth of what I advance.

(III.) Having now shown you the nature of and the descent of the Ancient Mysteries, which any one can prove for himself by a diligent study of old tomes, I will proceed to instruct you how Speculative Masonry assumed its present form. I do not altogether agree with the iconoclastic school. As various branches of Craft Masons in old times were instituted by various high-caste or professedly Theosophic systems, so they possessed more or less of their One learning. The fact that they used some of the same secret symbols (geometrical and otherwise) without understanding them, and, more or less, the same signs as the Mysteries, is proof that both associations had one and the same derivation. I believe that, owing to certain laws passed against the English operatives in the 15th century, politically to prevent their striking for higher wages by confederating in chapters, their system degenerated by the difficulty of their position; and, moreover, in England, as early as the year 1663, had become nearly extinct as a trade system, and lost its operative character by the admission of Rosicrucians, Geometricians, Alchemists, Theosophists, Knights of Malta, and other learned men and gentlemen of position. These, naturally, in their Lodge attendance brought into Craft Masonry the various dogmas and ceremonies with which they were acquainted (Rosicrucianism and Templary), out of which—by uniting, adapting, and amending—about the year 1686, sprang the Rite called Ancient Masonry, of seven degrees: virtually, three Craft degrees and three High degrees. At this time the leading spirit both in Craft Masonry and in Rosicrucianism was Elias Ashmole, and he kept a diary, from which we can gather that Father Backhouse was his teacher, and that both societies fell into decay together, and both revived together in 1682.* It is evident, therefore, that the Rosicrucians—who had too freely written upon their instruction, and met with ridicule—found the Operative Guild conveniently ready to their hand, and grafted upon it their own Mysteries. Also, from this time, Rosicrucianism disappears, and Freemasonry springs into life with all the possessions of the former. The public name of the brothers, as well as their secret language, has been in constant change; and in the course of time some disruptive

---

* The Diary of Elias Ashmole has been published.

cause will prostrate the popularity of Freemasonry, and our system will then assume, as the House of Wisdom, a new designation for the profane world.

It was in the year 1717 that the first Grand Lodge was formed at London, and the object of the promoters was to accept as little improvement as possible, and follow the old Operative lines. It can be proved* that there was in existence in 1717 certain Craft Lodges which had no participation in the formation of the Grand Lodge of London, and even the Grand Master was prohibited from visiting these lodges; and in 1738 the two systems—one of which recognised three degrees, called Modern Masonry, and the other seven degrees, called Ancient Masonry—came to wordy quarrels, leading to the establishment of a second London Grand Lodge. The Grand Lodge of All England, at York, took the part of the Ancients, and themselves practised the seven degree system; and there is a printed work of 1744 mentioning this fact. But we have, fortunately, a printed book, written in the year 1721, by Robert Samber, entitled "Long Livers," and couched entirely in the symbolical language of Alchemy and Rosicrucianism†—much of which our members can understand. In it we find mention of those Higher Mysteries which could only be conferred when the Craft Mason "had learned how to govern his tongue," and which, by the language used, are evidently (as they existed 50 years later) Arch, Templar, and Templar Priest. It is a symbolical history of Freemasonry from the creation; and it will please our members to learn that there is no Rite which, even at this distance of time, it will so well illustrate as our own. In France, there is a system practising our seven degrees, under the designation of Order of the Temple, and, though its charter from Jacques de Molay has been pronounced a forgery, the signature of Philip, Duke of Orleans, in 1705, is pronounced genuine. Moreover, in the year 1743, there existed in London a body claiming to date from time immemorial as a chapter of Heredom—Rosy Cross, or Templar. It had three grades: Arch, or Knight of the East, Rose Cross, and Mystic Point. The same degrees are minuted in 1746 as being practised in Durham. The Chevalier Ramsey, in France, was an active member of the Seven Degree Rite from 1728 to 1738. In 1736, according to Folger, but probably from 1725, the Grand Lodge of France had

---

* Leon Hyneman's "Ancient York and London Grand Lodges" (Philadelphia, 1872) treats upon a part of this subject.
† Reprinted by Brother George Kenning, in the *Freemasons' Magazine*.

appended to their Craft Warrant, obtained in 1725 from the 1717 Grand Lodge of London, the three grades of H.R.M., R.S.Y.-C.S.S., to which they added others; and Prince Charles Edward Stuart introduced them at Bordeaux in 1744, and gave a charter for the Rosy Cross to Arras in 1747 as Hereditary Grand Master, stating that previous to the misfortunes of his family it had been styled Knight of the Eagle and Pelican—our own badge, and the banner of his father in 1715. The Templar system of Von Marshall and Hunde sprang from them in 1740 and 1743, and at an early period they were introduced into Sweden. In Germany, in 1745, the High Grade system was Rosicrucian, and claimed derivation from the old society. The names of the brethren mentioned as practising these High Grades between 1728 and 1743 are men of high position, who vouched for their antiquity; and, moreover, the circumstances necessitate an origin not later than the year 1686, which was the date traditionally assigned upon certificates as the "year of revival" last century. What I contend for is that in England a High Grade Rite of seven degrees existed prior to the establishment of any Grand Lodge, and that such degrees were derived from the occult Rosicrucian School: that this system, in 1730, was known in England as Templars; in France, as Rosy Cross; in Sweden, as Royal Secret; and in Germany, as Rosicrucians. From this basis sprang numerous Orders, by which each author intended to develop his own special knowledge, and of which I will mention some only that bear upon our Antient and Primitive Masonry—the best of all the Masonic Rites, whether from its universality or its general features and its work. About the middle of the 18th century the Scottish Philosophical Rite, of eighteen degrees, was established at Marseilles; and about the same date Koppen established in Germany a Rite of African Architects, of which the fifth degree was Aletophilote, or Lover of Truth, a degree claiming to date from 1736, and afterwards introduced into the Rite of Perfection under the name of Prussian Noachite. But it is no part of my present purpose to expose the infamies of Lacorne, who, through Bonneville's Chapter of Clermont (the degrees of which are given as Knight of the Eagle, or Elect Master, Illustrious Knight, and Sublime Knight), established the Order of the East and West, of 25 degrees; nor will I dwell on the insane pretensions and forgeries of the Charleston Council, who concocted the new Ancient and Accepted Rite, after 1802.*

---

* Vide "Folger's History of the Ancient and Accepted Rite," republished in 1882, and the most learned and impartial work on the subject.

(IV.) The leading particulars of the High Grade Rites, of which I make no mention here, will be found in the history attached to the Statutes of our Antient and Primitive Rite of Masonry. The Rite which of all others most influenced the Masonry of last century was that of Martinez Paschalis, a German, born not later than 1728, who had obtained initiation into the Temple Mysteries of Turkey and Arabia, and who, returning from his travels, established the Rite of Elected Cohens, or Priests. The well-known Chevalier St. Martin took up his system, and the Rite of Primitive Philalethes, or Lovers of Truth, was established in 1773, and was identical in its aim with the Primitive Philadelphes, or Lovers of Mankind, which followed at Narbonne in 1779. It is especially to this Primitive Rite that we trace our own, and to the peculiarity of its organisation do we owe our numerous degrees. Writers have often been led into misconception by this peculiarity. The fact is that its *three* series and *seven* classes of defined degrees had the power of accepting and practising all systems. Ragon says that the Rite was formed of three classes of Masons, who received ten degrees of instruction; but that these ten degrees were not specifically fixed, but were the generic names of collections which need only to be developed to the utmost extent of which they were capable in order to evolve an infinite number of grades. Thus, the *first* series comprehended the three blue degrees; the *second* series has nominally three degrees, but the fourth degree rules two others; the fifth degree possessed one, and the sixth degree, Knight of the Sword (our Secret Vault), ruled two others—viz., Knight of the East (our Knight of the Sword), and Prince of Jerusalem (our Knight of Jerusalem). The *third* series of Rose Croix consisted of four chapters, and embraced all Masonic degrees and all Masonic knowledge and occult science.

It is believed that the Ancient Mysteries are yet practised in Egypt by certain Dervishes, and Napoleon the Great and Kleber, who were French Masons, received affiliation to the Egyptian by investure with a ring by an old Egyptian Sage, at the Great Pyramid of Cheops. Napoleon and the officers of his army, upon this, in 1798, established European Freemasonry with a Grand Lodge at Cairo, and, having initiated a brother named Samuel Honis, he reconveyed the present Rite of Memphis to France. It was in 1815 that certain travelled initiates, Frenchmen and Egyptians, of this Rite (Gabriel Matthieu Marconis de Negre, Grand Master and Hierophant; the Baron Dumas, the Marquis de Laroque, Samuel Honis, of Cairo, &c.) reconstituted a Grand Orient of it at Montauban, called Disciples of Memphis. The Egyptian Rite of Memphis continued to prosper, and when Mehemet Ali Pasha obtained the direction of affairs in Egypt he gave his patronage to the Lodges on Egyptian soil; they continued a correspondence by means of cyphers, yet preserved to us, with their confreres in Europe and the rest of the world. After the death of the great Pasha, the Rite of Memphis sank for awhile—perhaps in consequence of their meddling with politics—as it is asserted that in his time Greek and Arab women were members of the Lodges. The son of the first French Grand Hierophant, Jacques Etienne Marconis, a man of great learning and strict morals, and in every way an honour to Masonry, supported by his father, carried our Rite to Brussels in 1838, and to Paris in 1839, where he founded the Grand Lodge of Osiris, whence it spread again to Egypt, Italy, Roumania, and America. The Grand Orient, or Craft Grand Lodge of France, at that time the highest authority on High Grade Masonry in the world, secured the control of it in 1862, and we derive our own origin from them in that year. It is probably the only High Grade Rite which ever had its Charter ratified by a Grand Lodge of Symbolical or Craft Masons, and we can, therefore, ask Craft Masons to admit that we are the most legitimate of all existing Rites. We still, as of old, divide our system into three series and seven classes—representing Operative, Military, and Priestly Masonry—and we continue to give each of our Chapters, Senates, and Councils, under their respective warrants, power to confer any of the old Rites up to ninety degrees, as also the less valuable Rite of Mizraim. For the orders thus conferred we issue a separate certificate, and any brother who has not already been inducted into these additional degrees can be so on application, and at a trifling cost. In our system there is nothing to be found that is in any way antagonistic to Craft Masonry, *and we receive those only who have been raised as Master Masons under some constitutional Grand Lodge.* The Grand Lodge of England, at the union of the opposing Grand Lodges, in 1813, shut itself out for ever from recognising any degrees beyond the three first; but undertook, at the same time, to *allow any of its members to practise these Higher Mysteries.* The higher degrees of last century are no longer old English Masonry; the Arch and Templar degrees have been entirely changed, and the seventh degree, or Priest of the Temple of Holy Wisdom, termed the Seventh Pillar of the House, abandoned altogether: thus, pure Ancient Masonry has ceased to prevail under our Grand Lodge of England, and an entirely modern system has taken its place. Every degree, from the first to the ninetieth, has been the product of some private individual; where there is any choice of antiquity the preference lies with some of the Higher Mysteries : hence, if one is spurious—a common word in the mouth of the ignorant—all are spurious, including the first, second, and third degrees. It follows that the value of each degree of the ninety must be estimated by its beauty, its truth, and its morality, for Craft ceremonial has no higher antiquity than the High Grades. In this country Craft Masons, as a rule, decry the High Grades, because they are kept out of them until they apply in a constitutional way ; nor do they know their value as a system of instruction. But for the brother who travels they are a necessity, as abroad the mere Craft Mason is looked down upon as very low in the scale, and he has often to be requested to withdraw from the lodge—in the same way that a F.C. would be if a lodge of M.M. had to be opened. In a sense, it is possible that Craft Masonry may suffer by the fact that the High Grade Mason almost invariably becomes more attached to its ornate ceremonies than he has been to those of the Craft ; but, on the other hand, the Higher Mysteries act as an incentive to retain the M.M. in his allegiance, which, without them, he would have abandoned. In every way, the balance of wisdom is in favour of their zealous practice. They are a necessity for the polished and learned Mason, and it is better for the Craft itself that they should form a part of Freemasonry rather than break away from it and become a rival system, as was frequently the case in France and elsewhere. Essentially, the caste system exists *de facto* as much in this country as in India : the Craft Mason who joins his lodge to push his business, and only thinks of his pecuniary interests, is a natural-born Sudra, and will never be anything else ; he who aspires after divine treasure is a born Brahmin of the highest caste, and will knock at the door of our Temple for admission when he knows what we offer him.

I think you will admit that I have fulfilled the promises with which I set out, and have proved these things : first, that our present Craft Ceremonial, according to its best antiquaries, has no great antiquity ; second, that the High Grade *culte* is of immense age : third, I have shown the origin of the present system ; and, lastly, that the Antient and Primitive Rite of Masonry has special claims upon you.

And now, my brethren, before I bring my address to a close, it may be necessary to answer two possible—nay, probable—objections which may be raised when my statements permeate the Masonic family by the aid of that wing of God, the Press. The fanatical Craft Mason may say, as they have done, that my true history is an attack upon Symbolical Masonry. This is an idle objection. No one has more respect for our "mother" than have we; but the truth before all things: and Craft Masonry holds too high a position before the world to be influenced by points of origin and the value of certain elements which went to its formation—disputes which took place a century and a half ago. The fanatical religionist may say that there can come no good out of a system of High Grade *culte* which originated at the birth of humanity, and admits Masons of all religious opinions. Ah! how little such persons know what true religion is before God and man! St. Augustine, an initiate of the Gnostics, said that Christianity existed from the earliest period, and was in all ages present with the human race before Christ came in the flesh: and this is the Christianity which our Rite teaches. The dogmas of the seven-storied House of Wisdom, in all time, have been that of a pure life and devout practices, with prayer and meditation; and I may inform you that its Mysteries may appertain to the pure teachings of Zoroaster, Christna, Buddha, or Jesus: that is, you will understand, it is a system of provable philosophic ethics practised apart from the mere ceremonies of religion— general principles applicable to all faiths spread over the face of the world—Theosophical Masonry.

And now, in conclusion, I say to you, in the words of the Grand Hierophants of Egypt: "Mortals, whose eager lips aspire to suck the teats of Truth, learn that there exists but one sole Architect of this immense Temple called the Universe! . . . Go, spread upon earth, among the children of men, the sublime truths ye come hither to learn! but accord not this favour to the unworthy. Write not upon snow." Seek your proselytes amongst those only who can appreciate what we teach; we need not mere numbers. Bring to our folds those only who can raise their hearts to the divine. Tell them that we interfere neither with their Craft allegiance nor their religion. We come to our brethren guileless. We have no forged charters of great personages— no false history. We bind no one to our Councils with bands of iron, nor prohibit them from belonging to other systems. Freemasons—they come to us free, and they may depart free if they find that we do not satisfy their wants.

But let me emphatically urge you to brotherly firmness. Do not allow our beautiful and instructive Rite to be hindered and defamed by blind leaders of the blind, and by those who are interested in the propagation of pretentiously false systems, and who practically set brother against brother by pretending to high social position above the aspiration of the average Mason, and by requiring, as they do, certain religious tests and declarations. That is not Masonry. If these pretenders offer us open war or secret intrigue—as they have done, and may do again—let us proclaim in all lodges that we have far better right in Masonry, and in the highest offices of its councils, than have they; and call upon the offenders, whatever their boasted social position may be, to depart from a society which they pollute by their presence, and to whose brotherhood they do not merit to belong. Masonry is Truth, Love, Tolerance! Its converse is forgery and lies, unbrotherly acts, social and religious exclusiveness. We hope to represent in all senses the first series; let whoso will accept the latter. We are content to leave it to the Craft Universal to examine our respective claims, and to judge between us. Much as I esteem Craft Masonry, if I thought that it was possible as a society that it could listen to and encourage Masonic traitors, perjurers, and false traducers, I should say that it was the most base and vile of all societies: for it is in reality capable of effecting either great good or great harm, according as it is officered and directed by honourable or dishonourable brethren. Hence, it becomes the bounden duty of every Craft Mason, even if an opponent of the High Grades, to make assurance that the officers of the Craft are men of liberal and enlightened character, and of common honesty of purpose, who would shame to set Masons by the ears with social and religious tests and oaths. We are really fighting the battle of liberty for Craft Masonry at our own cost, and our brethren of the Craft do not require to be told that a false and spurious system of High Grade Masonry even now dominates all the acts of the Grand Lodge of London, to the detriment of all true Masonry, or advancement of the meritorious and modest brother: and hence, by supporting our Rite, the Craft declares itself emphatically for liberty of conscience, as in duty bound. Beyond this, we can have no wish to introduce the question of the High Grades into our Lodges.

# BIBLIOTHECA MASONICA

## F.L. Gardner

# A CATALOGUE RAISONNÉ

## OF WORKS ON THE

# OCCULT SCIENCES

BY

## F. LEIGH GARDNER

*Author of* "Rosicrucian Books," "Astrological Books," etc.

VOL. III.

## Freemasonry

*A CATALOGUE OF LODGE HISTORIES (ENGLAND)*

*with a PREFACE*

BY

## Dr. WILLIAM WYNN WESTCOTT,

P.M., P.G.D., P.Z., 30°

*(Supreme Magus of the Rosicrucians of England)*

London.
F. L. GARDNER,
14, Marlborough Road, Gunnersbury, W.

---

1912.

# BIBLIOTHECA MASONICA
F.L. Gardner

# PREFACE.

——:o:——

MY friend and fellow student, Mr. Frederick Leigh Gardner, has asked me to write a short introductory note to this Third Volume of his Bibliotheca. The first volume upon Rosicrucian and second upon Astrological Books have supplied in a very compendious and useful form, Catalogues of all available works on those subjects: under each heading were supplied the name of the Author and the full title of the book, with date and place of publication; while in numerous instances very interesting personal comments and antiquarian notes were added.

This present volume provides a very complete Catalogue of the Histories of English Freemasons' Lodges; it mentions in fact every such work as could be found after months of research.

Our late Brother, W. J. Hughan, the notable Masonic Historian, published many years ago (1892) a short list of Lodge Histories, but such works were at that time very few in comparison with the number which have since appeared.

The Masonic interest in these works depends greatly upon the antiquity of the Consecration of the Lodge referred to: the Minutes of the early years of our oldest Lodges contain many details of great interest, in regard to procedure, mode of constitution, the working of the several degrees and the powers of the Worshipful Master, and his Officers and of customs now long since abandoned.

Histories of Lodges of modern constitution rarely contain details of importance in regard to history or procedure, however interesting they may be to surviving brethren who are mentioned therein. For a great deal more than half a century

## PREFACE.

all English Lodges have been worked in almost strict accordance with the regulations of the Book of Constitutions, and so a narrative of their proceedings consists of little but business details, lists of names, and perhaps speeches of Masters and Grand Lodge Officers.

There still remain a great number of very old Lodges whose Histories have not yet been written, and although it is unfortunately true that in many instances the oldest Minute Books have been lost or destroyed, there are some Lodges whose records are extant and yet await a literary Past Master to edit and publish them. Our brethren should bear in mind that *all* missing records have not been destroyed although lost, and that such volumes *may* be recovered from old bookshops and the lumber rooms of country houses.

Some notes of interest in relation to old Lodges whose Histories have not yet been printed may be found scattered through the Masonic works of Brothers Oliver, Mackenzie, Hughan, Lane, Sadler, and also in the historical essays contributed to the many volumes of the "Ars Quatuor Coronatorum," edited by the late Brother G. W. Speth, and by our surviving Brothers W. H. Rylands and W. J. Songhurst.

It is a great source of pleasure to me that these volumes of the Bibliotheca Rosicruciana, Astrologica, and of English Lodge Histories should have been produced by my R. W. Frater Frederick Leigh Gardner, Hon. 9° and Past Secretary General of the Rosicrucian Society of England.

I am glad to say that a Fourth Volume, a Bibliotheca Alchymica, or Catalogue of all extant works treating of physical and spiritual Alchymy is in course of preparation, and I feel sure will be of the greatest value and the widest interest.

WILLIAM WYNN WESTCOTT, IX°.,
Supreme Magus, S.R.I.A.

# Bibliotheca Masonica.

### No. 1.

An Address delivered at the Centenary Meeting of the "**Grand Masters Lodge**," No. 1, London, June 20th, 1859, by Edward J. Powell, P.M. 4to. London, 1859. 36 *pp*.

History and Record of Members of "**Grand Masters Lodge**," No. 1, London, from 1759 to 1895, by Charles Belton, P.M. 8vo. London, 1895. 82 *pp*. *Second Edition*, 1897. 118 *pp*.

History and Records of Members of "**Grand Masters Lodge**," No. 1, London, from 1759 to 1904, *Third Edition*, by Charles Belton, P.M. 8vo. London, 1904. 142*pp*.

An old Atholl Lodge—Chartered August 13th, 1759.

### No. 2.

Records of the Lodge Original No. 1, now the "**Lodge of Antiquity**," No. 2, London, acting by Immemorial Constitution. Vol. 1 (all published), edited by W. H. Rylands, P.M. 4to. London. Illustrated. *Privately printed*, 1911, a handsome volume.

Collation (x) 434 *pp*.

Contains a beautifully executed facsimile of Arms at the beginning of the Roll of "Old Charges," A.D., 1686. The other Volumes will follow.

### No. 4.

History of "**Royal Somerset House and Inverness Lodge**," No. 4, London, as told by the Lodge Register, by G. Blizard Abbott. 8vo. London, 1891. 16 *pp*.

Reprinted from "The Freemason," Xmas, 1890.

An old Time Immemorial Lodge, originally No. 4, then No. 2, reverting again at the Union to No. 4.

### No. 6.

The Centenary of the "**Lodge of Friendship**," No. 6, London, by William Platt. 4to. London, N.D., (1867?). 38 *pp*.

> An old Lodge dating back to A.D. 1721, sometime known as No. 3 and then as No 6.

### No. 10.

A History of the "**Westminster and Keystone Lodge**," No. 10, London, from 1722 to 1905, compiled by J. W. Sleigh Godding, P.M. Illustrated. 8vo. Plymouth, 1907. (250 *Numbered Copies*.)

> Collation (xii) 291 *pp*.
>
> An old "Moderns" Lodge, warranted January 28th, 1722, as the "Tyrian" Lodge, No. 7, then it became No. 6 & 5 until the Union, when it became No. 10.

### No. 12.

A Short Sketch of the "**Fortitude and Old Cumberland Lodge**," No. 12, London, by R. F. Gould. 8vo. London, 1900. 4 *pp*.

> Reprinted from "The Freemason." June 30th, 1900.
>
> An old "Modern" Lodge dating back to A.D. 1723, sometime known as No. 6.

### No. 16.

History of the "**Royal Alpha Lodge**," No. 16, London, by Col. Shadwell H. Clerke. 8vo. London, 1891. 22 *pp*.

> Contains very fine portraits of the Royal Family, with a roll of members from 1818, it dates back to A.D. 1722, (then called "The Ionic Lodge" No. 9, and in 1740 it became No. 8) it traces its descent however from no less than five old lodges

### No. 19.

A Brief Sketch of the History of the "**Royal Athelstan Lodge**," No. 19, London, by Witham M. Bywater, P.M. 8vo. London, N.D. (1869). 20 *pp*.

> An old Atholl Lodge, constituted A.D. 1769 as No. 159, then it became No. 10, now No. 19.

### No. 20.

History of the "**Royal Kent Lodge of Antiquity**," No. 20, Chatham, Kent, by W. J. Hughan. 8vo. Dover, 1893.

History of the "**Royal Kent Lodge of Antiquity**," No. 20, Chatham, by Herbert F. Whyman, P.P.G.D. Illustrated. 4to. Maidstone, 1910. 68*pp*. *A handsome volume.*

> This is the oldest Provincial Lodge in England. Constituted A.D 1723, it held under the "Atholl" constitution as No. 13, then Nos. 12 and 10, and now No. 20.

### No. 21.

"**The Lodge of Emulation,**" No. 21, London. Some notices of its early History, its distinguished Members and the events connected with its career, by Brackstone Baker, P.G.D. *Privately circulated.* 12mo. London, (1872.) 30 *pp*.

History and Records of the "**Lodge of Emulation,**" No. 21, London, from 1723 to 1906, by Henry Sadler, P.M. Illustrated. 8vo. London, 1906.

Collation (x) 211 *pp*.

This is a much more comprehensive work than the preceding one, it is very voluminous, and beautifully got up. The Lodge dates back to 15th May, 1723, sometime known as No. 12, then No. 22, and now No 21. It was an old "Moderns" Lodge, and in 1783 was known as "The Mourning Bush Lodge."

### No. 22.

History of "**The Neptune Lodge,**" No. 22, London, 1757 to 1909, by F. W. Golby, P.M. *Privately printed.* 8vo. London, 1910.

Collation (xvi) 249 *pp* and 10 plates.

An old Atholl Lodge, warranted 7th December, 1752, originally Nos. 64, 13, 23, and now No. 22.

### No. 23.

Some Memorials of the "**Globe Lodge**" No. 23, London; with a sketch of the Origin and History of the Red Apron, by Henry Sadler, P.M. Illustrated. 8vo. London, 1904. (300 *copies.*)

Collation (viii) 92 *pp*.

An old "Moderns" Lodge dating from 1723, known as Nos. 14, 25 and now No. 23. A handsome volume, beautifully illustrated.

### No. 25.

A short History of the "**Robert Burns Lodge,**" No. 25, London, by Henry Sadler, P.M., with an account of the Centenary Celebration, October 10th, 1910. 8vo. 12 *pp*. and copy of warrant.

An old Atholl Lodge, warranted 1st June, 1755.

### No. 28.

History of the "**Old King's Arms Lodge,**" No. 28, London, 1725 to 1899, by Albert F. Calvert, W.M. Illustrated. 4to. London, 1899. *A handsome volume.*

Collation (xii) 141*pp*.

An old "Moderns" Lodge, started A.D. 1725, sometime No. 21, then Nos. 34, 30, and now No. 28.

## No. 31.

**History of the "United Industrious Lodge,"** No. 31, Canterbury, by W. J. Hughan. 8vo. 1894.

<small>An old Atholl Lodge, warranted A.D. 1753, sometime No. 24, then 37, 34, and now No. 31.</small>

## No. 33.

**History of the "Britannic Lodge,"** No. 33, London, from 1730 to 1870, prepared for the Centenary Festival, 11th March, 1870, by F. W. Shields, P.M. 8vo. London (1870). 8 *pp.*

<small>An old "Moderns" Lodge, started A.D. 1730, sometime No. 27, then 42. 38, and now No. 33.</small>

## No. 35.

**History of the "Medina Lodge,"** No. 35, Cowes, Isle of Wight. (1733 to 1756,) by W. J. Hughan. 8vo. London, 1889, 12 *pp.*

<small>This History originally appeared in the "Freemason," 1889.</small>

<small>An old "Moderns" Lodge, started A.D. 1733, sometime No. 31, then Nos. 48, 41 and now No. 35.</small>

## No. 37.

**History of the "Anchor and Hope Lodge,"** No. 37, Bolton, (warranted 23rd October, 1732) together with a complete roll of its members, from A.D. 1765, by George P. Brockbank, P.M., and James Newton, P.M., etc.; in commemoration of the sesqui-centennial of the Lodge, 23rd October, 1882. 8vo. Bolton, 1882. 82 *pp.* *Second Edition, revised* 1896. 130 *pp.*

**Continuation History of the "Anchor and Hope Lodge,"** No. 37, Bolton, by F. W. Brockbank, P.M. 8vo. Bolton, 1907. 29 *pp.*

<small>An old "Moderns" Lodge, sometime No. 33, then Nos. 51, 44, and now No. 37.</small>

## No. 38.

Old Chichester Lodges, by J. St. Clair, P.M. Printed for the **"Lodge of Union,"** No. 38, Chichester. 8vo. (1909.) 19 *pp.*

## No. 39.

**History of "St. John the Baptist Lodge,"** No. 39, Exeter, By-Laws, &c. 8vo. Exeter, 1884.

<small>Collation 33 (iv.) *pp.*</small>

<small>Contains a facsimile of the original warrant of this "Moderns" Lodge, 11th July, 1732, and a supplement by the Secretary, A Hope, entitled "Notes on an old Minute Book," 1891. 24 *pp.* This Lodge has the distinction of having the oldest original warrant in actual use of any Lodge whatever, sometime No. 35, it became Nos. 53, 16, and now No. 39.</small>

No. 39—*(continued.)*

History of "**St. John the Baptist Lodge**," No. 39, Exeter, by Andrew Hope, W.M. 8vo. Exeter, 1894. Four folding plates, 139 *pp*. *Another Edition*, 1906, (viii.), 131 *pp*.

## No. 41.

An abridged History of the "**Royal Cumberland Lodge**," No. 41, Bath, from the year A.D. 1732 (no prior records being available), together with a brief sketch of the condition of the craft some years prior to this date, by Thomas P. Ashley, P.M. 4to. Bath, 1873. 38 *pp*.

John Pine states that this Lodge was chartered May 18th, 1733, but the original warrant gives 26th April, and No. 113, then Nos. 101, 59, 49, 39, 36, 55, 48, and now No. 41.

## No. 42.

History of the "**Lodge of Relief**," No. 42, Bury, Lancashire, by Edward A. Evans, J.W., in commemoration of its sesqui-centennial, 3rd July, 1883, with notices by J. Newton, P.M. and G. P. Brockbank, W.M. 8vo. Bury, 1883. 96 *pp*.

This old "Moderns" Lodge was warranted 3rd July, 1733, sometime No. 37, then No 57, 50 and now No 42.

## No. 43.

Early Records of "**St. Paul's Lodge**," No. 43, Birmingham; extracted from the Minute Books, 1764 to 1863, by B. H. Joseph, P.M., and J. H. Boocock, Secretary. 8vo. (Birmingham, 1863.)

Collation (ii.) 54 (iii.) *pp*., and Portrait of R. W. Lord Leigh.

This old Lodge was founded A.D. 1733, and in 1764 the Lodge Records prove that the members of the original Lodge of 1733 (Moderns) had petitioned for and obtained a warrant, No. 124, from the "Ancients"!!!

## No. 44.

A Brief Sketch of the "**Lodge of Friendship**," No. 44, Manchester, by Nathan Heywood, P.M. 8vo. Manchester, 1895.

Bye-laws and History of the "**Lodge of Friendship**," No. 44, Manchester, by Nathan Heywood, P.M. Coloured plate. 8vo. Manchester, 1901. 23 *pp*.

An old Atholl Lodge, warranted 18th June, 1755, as No 39 "St. Ann's Church and Mitre Lodge," at the Union it became Nos 59, 52, and now No. 44.

### No. 45.

A History of the "**Strong Man Lodge**," No. 45, London, by F. W. Driver, P.M. 4to. London, 1904.

Collation (iv) 88 pp

An old "Moderns" Lodge, constituted A.D. 1733.

### No. 48.

History of the "**Lodge of Industry**," No. 48, Gateshead-on-Tyne, 12mo., 1870, 24 pp., and Celebration of the 150th Anniversary of its connection with the Grand Lodge of England. Sketch of the Lodge by R. B. Reid, P.M. 12mo. Newcastle-on-Tyne. 1886. 32 pp.

The Earliest Records of this old "Moderns" Lodge commence on 29th September, 1725.

### No. 50.

The early History (1803 to 1859), of the "**Knights of Malta Lodge**," (formerly Nos. 47, 66 and 58), No. 50, Hinckley, Leicestershire, compiled from the Lodge Records and other authentic sources, by John T. Thorp. 6 plates. 8vo. Leicester, 1899. 89 pp.

### No. 51.

History and Bye-Laws of the "**Angel Lodge**," No 51, Colchester. 32mo. 1873. 42 pp.

This old Lodge was founded A.D. 1735, the History occupies 6 pp.

### No. 52.

History of "**Union Lodge**," No. 52, Norwich, by two of its Past Masters, Lord Amherst, of Hackney, P.G.W., and Hamon Le Strange, P.G.D. *Privately printed*, 4th March, 1898. Fine facsimile of warrant. A handsome volume.

Collations (viii) 158 pp

The earliest records in "Grand Lodge" appear on 27th December, 1736.

### No. 56.

Records of the "**Howard Lodge of Brotherly Love**," No. 56, London and Arundel, 1777-1821, by W. J. Hughan. 8vo. London, 1895. 8 pp.

A History of the "**Howard Lodge of Brotherly Love**." No. 56, Arundel, Sussex, constituted 21st December, 1736. A memorial of the Centenary Festival, 19th December, 1878, by Thomas Francis, W.M. 8vo. Portsmouth, 1883. 58 pp. *Second Edition*, 1898. 60 pp.

### No. 57.

A History of the warant of the "**Humber Lodge**," No. 65, (now No. 57), Hull, by J. Coltman Smith, P.M. 8vo. Hull, 1855. 36 pp.

A History of the "**Humber Lodge**," No. 57, Hull, by George A. Shaw, P.M. Illustrated. 8vo. London, N.D., (1910 ?).

Collation (xii) 176 pp

An old Atholl Lodge, warranted as No 53, A.D., 1756, and again on 17th April, 1775.

### No. 58.

History of the "**Lodge of Felicity**," No. 162 (now No. 58) London, from A.D. 1737 to 1887, with comments on contemporary events, by Wm. Smithett. 4to. London, 1887.

Collation (viii) 140 pp.

*Second Edition* with facsimile of *Constitution*, 24th August, 1737. 4to. London, 1891.

Collation (viii) 144 pp.

### No. 60.

"**Peace and Harmony Lodge**," No. 172, London, now (No. 60). Celebration of 150th Anniversary, 3rd May, 1888 (by F. Binckes). 4to. London, 1888. 20 pp.

A fine old Lodge History, with facsimile of its warrant, &c., 3rd May, 1738.

### No. 61.

History of the "**Lodge of Probity**," No. 61, Halifax, Yorks, and of the formation of the Provincial Grand Lodge of West Yorkshire and the Lodge of Promulgation, by Herbert Crossley, S.W. Illustrated. 8vo. Halifax, 1888. 336 pp.

### No. 63.

"**St. Mary's Lodge**," No. 63, London. Chronological Record from its constitution A.D. 1757, to its Centenary Festival, in A.D. 1857, by F. A. Winsor, P.M.; continued to the present time by W. Hollingworth, P.M., &c., with an account of Freemasonry in Germany, by E. E. Wendt. The whole Edited and Revised by Bros. Kelly and Hollingworth. 8vo. London, 1883. 120 pp.

"**St. Mary's Lodge**," No. 63, London, Chronological Record from the constitution in 1757 to the Centenary Festival in 1857, by Frederick A. Winsor, P.M.; continued from 1857 to 1882, by Wilmer Hollingworth, P.M.; and from 1882 to the 150th Anniversary Festival in 1907, by Cole A. Adams, P.M. 8vo. London, 1908. 128 pp. and 5 plates.

### No. 64.

By-Laws of the "**Lodge of Fortitude**," No. 64, Manchester, with copy of warrant (1st May, 1772) and a short historical account from 1860 to the present time, etc., by G. P. Brockbank, Secretary. 8vo. Bolton, 1888. 16 *pp*. *Another Edition* by H. Longman. 8vo. Lancaster, 1895.

This old Lodge was constituted 9th January, 1739.

### No. 65.

A History of the "**Lodge of Prosperity**," No. 65, London, by C. E. Ferry, P.M. Portrait. 8vo. London, 1884.

Collation (iv), 138 *pp*.

*Second Edition.* Enlarged. 4to. London, 1893.

Collation (iv), 130 *pp*., 8 plates.

### No. 69.

History of the "**Lodge of Unity**," No. 69, London, together with By-Laws and a note on Freemasons in the Eighteenth Century. 4to. London, 1901.

Collation (vi) 75 *pp*., and Reprint of Charter, 1824.

A Joint Committee of Bros R J Reece, E. H. Cartwright and G. F. Marshall, Past Masters, were entrusted with the production of this work. An old "Moderns" Lodge, founded 1742

### No. 72.

[A History of the] "**Royal Jubilee Lodge**," No. 72, London, by Henry A. Darch, P M. *Printed for private circulation,* 1910.

Collation (ii), 45 *pp*., 7 plates.

### No. 73.

The Address given in commemoration of the Centenary of "**Mount Lebanon Lodge**," No. 73, London, by John Dixon, M.D., 15th January, 1878. 12mo. London, 26 *pp*.

This old Lodge was founded A.D. 1760.

### No. 75.

A Brief Sketch of the "**Lodge of Love and Honour**," No. 75, Falmouth, by W. J. Hughan, P.S.G.D. 16mo. Falmouth, 1877. 28 *pp*. *Another Edition,* 1888. 35 *pp*.

### No. 76.

Extracts from the Minute Books of the "**Lodge of Economy**," No. 76, Winchester, 1761 to 1887, by T. Stopher, W.M. 4to. Winchester, Hants, 1887.

Collation (vi) 30 *pp*.

This old Lodge was warranted 9th January, 1761.

### No. 78.

A brief History of the "**Imperial George Lodge**," No. 78, Middleton, Lancashire, by Samuel Hewitt. 12mo. Manchester, N.D., (1879). 20 *pp*.

### No. 80.

History of the "**St. John's Lodge**," No. 80, Sunderland, by William Logan, P.M. 8vo. Sunderland, 1889. 14 *pp*.

An old Atholl Lodge, warranted October 21st, 1761.

### No. 84.

History of "**Doyle's Lodge of Fellowship**," No. 84, Guernsey, by W. T. Kinnersley, W.M. 8vo. Guernsey, 1873.

Collation, 52 (xxx) *pp*.

The articles of Union, 25th November, 1813, are reproduced in the appendix.

### No. 88.

"**Scientific Lodge**," No. 88, Cambridge, Our Early Days, by Arthur K. Hill, P.M. *For private circulation only.* 8vo. Cambridge, 1902.

Collation (v), 25 *pp*.

### No. 94.

History of the "**Phœnix Lodge**," No. 94, Sunderland, from the Consecration 1755 to 1905, compiled by Thomas O. Todd, P.M. Illustrated. 8vo. Sunderland, 1906. 179 *pp*.

### No. 99.

The History of "**The Shakespear Lodge**," No. 99, (formerly No. 221), 1757 to 1904, by Ernest A. Ebblewhite, W.M. Illustrated. 4to. London. *Privately printed* 1905. (150 numbered copies.) A handsome volume.

Collation (xvi) 444 *pp*.

This old Lodge was warranted 15th February, 1757.

### No. 100.

A Short History of "**Friendship Lodge**," No. 100, Great Yarmouth, by A. E. Richmond, W.M. 32mo. N.D., 1909. 20 *pp*.

An old warranted Lodge, A.D. 1757.

### No. 104.

Centenary of "**St. John's Lodge**," No 104, Stockport, 13th November, 1865. A Short History of the Lodge and its connection with Ancient Freemasonry, by John Walsh, S.D. 12mo. Manchester (1865). 16 *pp*. *Another Edition*, by John Crennell. 12mo. Stockport, 1893. 144 *pp*.

Constituted A.D. 1765, as No. 139 "Antients."

### No. 107.

History of "**Philanthropic Lodge**," No. 107, King's Lynn, compiled by J. S. B. Glasier, P.M., on the occasion of its Centenary Anniversary, 22nd March, 1910. Illustrated. 4to. King's Lynn, 1911. 176 *pp*. *A handsome volume, privately printed*.

### No. 112.

Notes from the old Records of "**St George's Lodge**," No. 112, Exeter, compiled by Commander Claude Plenderleath, Secretary. 8vo. 1909. 29 *pp*.

### No. 114.

Bye-Laws of the "**British Union Lodge**." No. 114, Ipswich, to which is prefixed a brief History of the Lodge, &c. 12mo. (Ipswich) 1885. 24 *pp*.

Another History appeared in the "Masonic Magazine" for 1875-76, and again in a work by E. Holmes, called "Tales, Poems and Masonic Papers," printed at Stokesley 12mo. 1877.

### No. 117.

"**The Salopian Lodge of Charity**," No. 117. Shrewsbury; A monograph by C. H. Cowling. 8vo. Shrewsbury, 1898.

### No. 119.

The Dispute about the Age of the "**Sun, Square, and Compasses Lodge**." No. 119. Whitehaven. 8vo. 1890.

Warranted by the Antients, May 18th, 1768, as No 157.

### No. 124.

History of Freemasonry in the City of Durham, in connection with the "**Marquis of Granby Lodge**," No. 124, by William Logan, P.M. 8vo. London, 1886.

Collation (x) 108 *pp.*

An old Lodge, warranted 8th September, 1763; its Records commence 24th June, 1738 and it has the enviable distinction of the oldest " Mark " Records. viz.: A.D. 1773 to 1777.

### No. 131.

Brief Sketch of "**Fortitude Lodge**," No. 131, Truro, with Bye-Laws, &c., by W. J. Hughan. 12mo. Truro. 34 *pp.*

An old Atholl Lodge, warranted 6th July, 1772.

### No. 133.

Freemasory in Faversham, 1763 to 1887. [History of the "**Harmony Lodge**," No. 133.] Copies of warrants, &c., collected and arranged by Francis F. Giraud. 8vo. Faversham, 1887. 27 *pp.* (*Private circulation.*)

An old Lodge, bearing a warrant dated 28th August, 1764.

Freemasonry in Faversham, 1763 to 1899, by F. F. Giraud. *Second Edition. Privately printed.* 8vo. Margate, 1900. 56 *pp.*

### No. 134.

A Short History of "**The Caledonian Lodge**," No. 134, London, by Fred J. W. Crowe. Illustrated. 8vo. London, 1910. 12 *pp.*

This is a Reprint from "The Freemason," 1910.

An old Atholl Lodge, dating back to A.D. 1764.

### No. 137.

Freemasonry in Poole, being a History of the "**Lodge of Amity**," No. 137, Poole, Dorset, (1765 to 1897), and of the R.A. Chapter No. 137, with a sketch of the Amity Mark Lodge, No. 132, compiled by Alexander C. Chapin, P.M. Portrait of T. Dunckerley. 8vo. Poole and London, 1897.

Collation (x) 141 *pp.*

This Lodge was warranted A.D. 1765.

### No. 142.

By-Laws and Historical Notice of "**St. Thomas's Lodge**," No. 142 (originally No. 193,) London. Post, 4to. (London), 1907.

Collation 70 (vii) *pp.*

An old Atholl Lodge, warranted 11th May, 1775, and very possibly earlier—(June 14th, 1756.)

### No. 145.

Historic Records of the "**Lodge of Prudent Brethren**," No. 145, London, by Harry Guy, P.M. 32mo. London, 1906. 52 *pp*. An Appendix appeared in 1908. 20 *pp*.

An old Atholl Lodge, constituted 1775 as No. 195, then Nos. 241, 169 and now No. 145.

### No. 146.

History of the "**Lodge of Antiquity**," No. 146, Bolton, by James Newton, P.M. 8vo. Bolton, 1882. 76 *pp*.

An old Lodge, warranted 24th June, 1776.

### No. 157.

Records of the Craft, Memoranda of the "**Bedford Lodge**," No. 183 (now 157) 1776 to 1844, by Messrs. J. Harris and A. Thrupp, Secretaries.

This appeared in "*The Rosicrucian*," January, 1876.

### No. 162.

A few notes about the "**Cadogan Lodge**," No. 162, London, compiled from its Records by Hildebrand Ramsden, P.M. 32mo. London, 1881. 32 *pp*.

An old Lodge, warranted 9th February, 1767.

### No. 170.

Historic Notes of "**All Soul's Lodge**," No. 170, Weymouth, 1767 to 1895, by Zillwood Milledge, P.M. Illustrated. 8vo. Weymouth, 1896.

Collation (xviii) 350 *pp*. and Errata.

### No. 173.

"**The Phœnix Lodge**," No. 173, London, 1785 to 1909. A retrospect, 4 plates and portraits. 8vo. London, 1910. (*For Private Circulation only.*)

Collation (viii) 76 *pp*.

### No. 174.

A History of the "**Lodge of Sincerity**," No. 174, London, compiled from its Minutes, 1784-1887, by John Newton, P.M. Portrait, &c. 8vo. London, 1888.

Collation (viii), 126 *pp*.

This Lodge was warranted A.D. 1768.

### No. 176.

The Origin and History of an old Masonic Lodge "**The Caveac**," No. 176, by John P. Simpson, P.M. etc. Illustrated. 8vo. London, 1905, and a *Supplement*, N.D., (1907 ?). 7 *pp.*
Collation (vi) 89 *pp.*

### No. 177.

History of the "**Domatic Lodge**," No. 177. London, 1786 to 1886, written for the Centenary Festival, 12 February, 1886, by G. B. Abbott. 8vo. London, 1886.
Collation 43 (xx) *pp.*

An old warranted Lodge, 7th February, 1786, formerly known as the "*Deomatic Lodge*," No. 234.

### No 178.

Masonry in Wigan ; being a Brief History of the "**Lodge of Antiquity**," No. 235, (now No. 178), with references to other Lodges in the Borough at the close of the last and beginning of the present century, by J. Brown, Secretary. 8vo. Wigan, 1882. 66 *pp.*

An old Lodge, warranted 26th May, 1786.

### No. 183.

The History of the "**Lodge of Unity**," No. 183, London (formerly Nos. 441, 376, 289, 290, 242, 305, 215), extracted from the Minutes and other Documents of the Lodge, and from the Records and Register of Grand Lodge, by George W. Speth, P.M. 8vo. London, 1881.
Collation 44 (xvi) *pp.* and two folding tables.

### No. 185.

History of the "**Lodge of Tranquillity**," No. 185, London, from its origin to the present time, by John Constable, W.M., with appendices, etc. 8vo. London, 1874.
Collation (viii) 71 *pp.* and one folding plate of Warrant.

The list of members dates back as far as A.D. 1787, and my own father's name is amongst them, i.e. Frederick Gardner, October 20th, 1873.

### No. 189.

Bye-Laws and History of "**Lodge Sincerity**," No. 189, Stonehouse, Plymouth, by M(artin) G(eorge) E(ndle), P.M., and L(ovell) R(edmore) D(unstan), W.M. *For private circulation only.* 8vo. Plymouth, 1909. 34 *pp.*

## No. 191.

"**Lodge of St. John**," No. 191, Bury, Lancashire, Centenary Festival, &c.. June 24th, 1869. 8vo. Bury, 1869. 32 pp.

It contains hardly any account of the Lodge History.

## No. 192.

History of the "**Lion and Lamb Lodge**," No. 192, London, 1789-1899, by George Abbott, P.M. Written in commemoration of the Centenary of the Lodge, 24th December, 1899. 8vo. London (1890). 42 pp.

History of the "**Lion and Lamb Lodge**," No. 192, London, by W. J. Hughan. Fine coloured plates. 8vo. London, 1894. 192 pp.

This old Lodge was warranted 24th December, 1789.

## No. 195.

History of the "**Lodge of Hengist**," No. 195, Bournemouth, 1770 to 1870. A paper read at the Centenary Festival, 23rd November, 1870, by Revd. P. H. Newnham, W.M. 12mo. Bournemouth and London (1870). 38 pp and tables.

History of the "**Lodge of Hengist**," No. 195, Bournemouth, numerous illustrations (20) and appendices, by C. J. Whitting, W.M. *Second Edition.* 8vo. Bournemouth and London, 1897.

Collation (xii) 272 pp.

The Lodge warrant is dated 23rd November, 1770.

## No. 197.

Centenary Celebration and History of the "**Jerusalem Lodge**," No. 197, London, 24th February, 1871. 4to. London, 1871. 56 pp.

Record of Celebration was written by C. E. Hollingsworth, and the Lodge History by Sir J. B. Monckton, P.G.W., &c.

## No. 198.

Some account of the "**Percy Lodge**" of Freemasons, No. 198, London, by George Cowell, P.M. Printed under the authority of the Lodge. Illustrated. 8vo. London, 1902.

Collation (vi) 73 pp.

## No. 204.

Centenary Records, 1802 to 1902, of the "**Caledonian Lodge**," No. 204, Manchester, compiled and Edited from Minute Books, M.SS., &c., by Alfred Ingham, P.M. 8v. Manchester, 1903. 4 plates. 95 pp.

### No. 211.

History of the "**St. Michael's Lodge,**" No. 211, London, compiled from such Minute Books as have been preserved (by W. W. Morgan, P.M.) 12mo. London, 1881.

Collation (iv) 44 *pp*.

This is a Reprint from the "Freemason's Chronicle"; the Lodge was warranted 11th September, 1795

### No. 214.

A Sketch of the History of the "**Lodge of Hope and Unity,**" No. 214, Brentwood, Essex, 1795 to 1895. 16mo. London, 1895. 22 *pp*.

An old Atholl Lodge, dated 3rd November, 1795.

### No. 216.

History and Records of the "**Harmonic Lodge,**" No. 216, Liverpool (formerly "Ancient," No. 299, "Union," No. 380 and 263) and the "Sacred Delta," Royal Arch Chapter by John Hawkins, P.M. 8vo. Liverpool, 1890.

Collation (iv) 120 *pp*.

This Lodge was warranted 22nd April, 1796.

### No. 217.

A History of "**Stability Lodge,**" No. 217, London, from 1797 to 1897, by Wm. Robert Smith. 8vo. London, 1897. *Not Published.*

Collation (vii) 40 *pp*.

An old Atholl Lodge, warranted October 10th, 1787.

### No. 221.

"**St. John's Lodge,**" No. 221, Bolton. A short History and Extracts from the old Minute Books, &c., by G. P. Brockbank, P.M. Tables, &c. 8vo. Bolton, 1880. 62 *pp*.

### No. 223.

Historical Notes and By-Laws of the "**Lodge Charity,**" No. 223, Plymouth, with a list of Worshipful Masters, &c., by Wm. Browning. 24mo. (Plymouth) 1892. 32 *pp*.

An old Atholl Lodge, warranted 1797.

### No. 227.

A short account of some of the History of the "**Ionic Lodge,**" No. 227, London, by John Songhurst. Folio. Margate, 1903.

An old Atholl Lodge, warranted 25th April, 1810

This account appeared in the A.Q.C. Transactions Vol. XVI. *pp*. 201-2.

### No. 228.

Lodge of "**United Strength**," No. 228, London, some particulars of its career as "Ancient" Lodge, No. 314, 1798 to 1813, by G. Blizard Abbott, P.M. 8vo. London, 1899.
Collation (v) 21 *pp* and 1 plate.

### No. 235.

A Centennial Sketch of the History of the Lodge of the "**Nine Muses**," No. 235, London, 1777 to 1877. Presented to the Brethren at the Centennial Festival, 8th May, 1877, by Walter Webb, W.M. 8vo. (London, 1877). 48 *pp*.
A warranted Lodge, 25th March, 1777.

### No. 236.

By-Laws, &c., to which is added a Short History of the "**York Lodge**," No. 236, (by Joseph Todd, P.M.) and of the "Grand Lodge of all England," York, (by William Cowling, P.M.) Portrait. 8vo. York, 1875. 50 *pp*.

The By-Laws of the "**York Lodge**." No. 236, York, together with a History of the Lodge and the "Ancient Grand Lodge of All England. 8vo. York, 1910. 52 *pp*.
This Edition has been Revised, brought up-to-date and re-written in parts.

### No. 237.

History and Bye-Laws of the "**Indefatigable Lodge**," No. 237, Swansea, from 1804 to 1888, with Bye-Laws, etc., by David Williams. 12mo. Swansea, 1888. 18 *pp*.

### No. 238.

St. Joh-Loge "**Der Pilger**," No. 238, London. Centenary Festival held at Freemason's Hall, London, 1st October, 1879, with a History of the Lodge, by Karl Bergmann, P.M. (*German Text*) 8vo. London, 1879.
Collation (ii) 52 *pp*.

Zur Feier des 125ten Gründungs-Festes der "**Pilgerloge**," No. 238 13th October, 1904, by Otto Hehner, P.M. 2 vols. 8vo. London, 1904.
Collations Vol. I. 24 (x) *pp*. and 1 Folding Table.
Vol. II. contains 22 loose portraits in a case.

### No. 240.

Report of Centenary Festival of "**St Hilda's Lodge**," No. 240, South Shields, and Brief History, compiled from the Minute Books for 100 years, by J. H. Thompson, S.D. 12mo. 1880. 40 *pp*.

### No. 241.

Programme of the celebration of the Centenary of the "**Merchant's Lodge**," No. 241, Liverpool, at the Masonic Hall, 22, Hope Street, Liverpool, 16th June, 1880. 15 *pp*.

### No. 242.

The Records of "**St. George's Lodge**," No. 242, Doncaster, giving every Minute of Importance from its foundation, with an account of the Centenary Celebration, &c., by William Delanoy, P.M. 4to. Doncaster, 1880. 102 *pp*. *Another Edition*, 1882. 104 *pp*.

The warrant is dated 11th July, 1780.

### No. 246.

"**The Royal Union Lodge**," No. 246, Cheltenham, 1813 to 1888. A Sketch of its History, compiled from the Lodge Minutes and Contemporary sources, by George Norman, P.M. Illustrated. 4to. (Cheltenham, 1888). *Privately circulated*.

Collation (xvi) 66 (xxiv) *pp*.

### No. 248.

Freemasonry in Brixham, Devon, 1781 to 1840 [or a Short History of the "**True Love and Unity Lodge**," No. 248, Brixham], by Fred J. W. Crowe. Folio. Margate, 1895. 71 *pp*.

This is a Reprint from the A.Q.C Lodge transactions for 1895.

### No. 250.

A Sketch of the History of the "**Minerva Lodge**," No. 250, Hull, read at the Centenary Festival, 8th October, 1883, by M. C. Peck, P.M. 12mo. (Hull, 1884). 52 *pp*. *An earlier Edition appeared in* 1878.

This is contained in a publication called "The Minerva Lodge Directory," 1884; it also appeared in subsequent Editions.

### No. 253.

The Centenary Celebration of the "**Tyrian Lodge**," No. 253, Derby, held at the Masonic Hall, 9th April, 1885, with a Sketch of the History of the Lodge for the Century, brief Annals, Lists of Members and Worshipful Masters. 8vo. Derby (1885). 74 *pp*.

The warrant is dated 26th March, 1785.

## No. 255.

A Short Account of the "**Lodge of Harmony**," No. 255, Richmond, Surrey, since its Revival in 1801, &c., by Gordon W. Clark, P.M. 8vo. 1868. *Second Edition* by Raymond H. Krupp, P.M. 12mo. (Richmond) 1885. 24 *pp*.

## No. 256.

Annals of the "**Lodge of Unions**," No. 256, London, from 1785 to 1885; compiled from the Minute Books by Reuben R. Davis, P.M. Illustrated. *Privately circulated*. A handsome volume. 4to. London, 1885.

Collation (vi) 176 *pp*.

[**Lodge of Unions.**] Illustrated History of the "**Emulation Lodge of Improvement**," No. 256, 1823 to 1903, with Brief Historical Sketches of its branches and offshoots, by Henry Sadler, P.M., etc. Illustrated. 8vo. London, 1904.

Collation (x) 217 *pp*.

## No. 257.

History of the "**Phœnix Lodge**," No. 257 Portsmouth 1786 to 1893, and the Chapter of Friendship, No. 257 1769 to 1893, &c., by Alexander Howell, P.M. Illustrated. *Privately printed*. 4to. Portsmouth, 1894. A handsome volume.

Collation (xiii) 273 *pp*.

## No. 259.

"**Prince of Wales's Lodge**," No. 259, London. List of Members from the time of its Constitution, with Notes of Proceedings and Circumstances of Interest in connection with the Lodge and its Members, compiled from the Minutes and other sources, by Thomas Fenn, P.M. 8vo. London, 1869. *Second Edition*, 1876. 56 *pp*. *Third Edition*, 1890. 104 *pp*.

## No. 262.

A History of Freemasonry in the Province of Shropshire, and of the "**Salopian Lodge**," No. 262, by Alexander Graham. 8vo. Shrewsbury, 1892.

Collation (xv) 232 *pp*.

An old "Moderns" Lodge, Warranted May 10th, 1727.

### No. 265.

History of the "**Royal Yorkshire Lodge**," No. 265, Keighley, (constituted No. 530 A.D. 1788), including an account of the Proceedings connected with the Celebration of the Centenary in 1888, by J. Ramsden Riley. *Privately printed.* Illustrated. 8vo. Keighley, 1889.

Collation (viii) 92 *pp.*

### No. 277.

"**Lodge of Friendship**," No. 277, Oldham, extracts from the Minutes with notes, a list of members, etc., by Rev. Joseph Harrison, M.A. 8vo. London, 1880. 18 *pp.* *Another Edition* by Rev. J. O. Jelly. 8vo. Oldham, 1891. 72 *pp.*

Reprinted from the "*Masonic Magazine*" 1880, with additions.

### No. 279.

An Introductory Sketch of the History of the "**St. John's Lodge**," No. 279, Leicester, by William Kelly, P.P.G.M., with By-Laws, &c. 12mo. (Leicester) 1888. 30 *pp.*

Centenary Celebration of "**St. John's Lodge**," No. 279, Leicester, Province of Leicestershire and Rutland, and a brief account of the Lodge from 1790 to 1890, by Maurice Williams, P.M., &c. Illustrated. 8vo. Leicester, 1892. 133 *pp.*

### No. 280.

Reminiscences of the "**Worcester Lodge**," No. 280, and of other Masonic Institutions in the Province and City of Worcester, by C. C. Whitney Griffiths, P.M. Published by the Lodge for Presentation only. 8vo. 1870. (viii) 16 *pp.*, 39 *pp.*, 6 *pp.*, 17 *pp.* Supplement to above (1872), 64 *pp.*

### No. 281.

The Earlier Years of "**Fortitude**," a paper read before the "**Lodge of Fortitude**," No. 281, Lancaster, on 9th February, 1887, by H. Longman, P.M. *Printed by special request.* 16mo. Lancaster, 1887. 20 *pp.*

Proceedings of the Centenary Meeting of the "**Lodge of Fortitude**," No. 281, Lancaster (November 16th, 1889). 32mo. 16 *pp.*

Records (1789-1889) of the "**Lodge of Fortitude**," Lancaster, numbered 573 484, 527, 350, and now 281. Compiled from the Minute Books by H. Longman, P.P.G.S. 8vo. Lancaster, 1895.

Collation (vii) 89 *pp.*

### No. 287.

An Historical Sketch of the "**Lodge of Unanimity**," No. 287, Stockport, with an account of the Centenary Celebration, September 14th, 1892, by James Cookson, P.M. and R. C. Blakehurst, P.M. 8vo. Stockport, 1892. Portrait, &c. 68 *pp*.

Originally No. 509 "Beneficient," then No. 543 "Unanimity," and now No. 287.

### No. 289.

History of the "**Lodge of Fidelity**," No. 289, Leeds, from 1792 to 1893, including a short account of Freemasonry in Leeds during the eighteenth century, and of the Principal Grand Lodges of the County of York and of the West Riding of Yorkshire, by Alfred Scarth, P.M., and Charles A. Braim, P.M. 4to. Leeds, 1894. (250 *copies*).

Collation (xx) 240 *pp*.

Copy of warrant, 24th September, 1792.

### No. 290.

The History of the "**Huddersfield Lodge**," No. 290, from 1793 to 1893, also the Centennial Celebration, by W. L. Wilmshurst. W.M. 4to. Huddersfield, 1893.

Collation 51 (iii) *pp*.

Centenary Record 23 *pp*.

In the early days, Certificates were given by the Master and Wardens of Lodges and *not* as now, by the Grand Lodge.

### No. 291.

History of the "**Rural Philanthropic Lodge**," No. 291, Highbridge, by Thomas F. Norris, P.M. 4to. Taunton, 1893. 47 *pp*.

Warrant dated 1793, signed by Thos Dunckerley.

### No. 294.

The Records of the "**Constitutional Lodge**," No. 294, Beverley, Yorkshire, giving Extracts from its Minutes in each year from the foundation in 1793, and details of the Centenary Celebration. 8vo. Beverley, Yorkshire, 1893. 38 *pp*.

### No. 295.

A Hundred Years' History of "**Combermere Lodge of Union**," No. 295, Macclesfield; also the Centenary Festival by R. Brown, P.M. 8vo. Macclesfield, 1893.

Collation (iv) 74 *pp*.

### No. 296.

History of the "**Royal Brunswick Lodge**," No. 296, Sheffield, by W. H. Stacey. 8vo. Sheffield, 1893. 93 *pp*.

An old Atholl Lodge, warranted 1776.

### No. 297.

Brief History of the "**Witham Lodge**," No. 374 (now No. 297), holden in the City of Lincoln, with a description of the Ceremonial used at the levelling of the Foundation Stone of a Masonic Hall and the Sermon preached by Rev. George Oliver. 8vo. London, 1841. 48 *pp*.

Contains references to the old extinct " Witham Lodge."

### No 298.

Memorials of the "**Lodge of Harmony**," No. 298, Rochdale, (originally No. 552 then Nos. 559 and 375) with some account of its Centenary Commemoration 7th December, 1893. Compiled from the Lodge Records and other sources, by Robinson Greenwood, S.D., and Robert R. Grey, P.M. 8vo. Rochdale, 1894.

Collation (vi) 64 *pp*.

### No. 300.

The Centenary Festival of the "**Lodge Minerva**," No. 300, Ashton-under-Lyne, 1794-1894. 8vo., 1st January, 1894. 29 *pp*.

The old Notes and History (although not so stated on the title page) commence from February 9th, 1797.

### No. 301.

Some Notes on the History of the "**Apollo Lodge**," No. 301, Alcester, 1794 to 1906, by D'Arcy Power, P.M. 4to. Birmingham (1906). 55 *pp*. and 5 plates. *A handsome volume.*

Founded at Alcester; warranted 26th February, 1794.

### No. 302.

Short History of the "**Lodge of Hope**," No. 302, Bradford, 1794 to 1894, written for the proceedings in Celebration of the Centenary of the Lodge, by Charles Gott, P.M., &c. 4to. Bradford, April, 1894. 21 *pp*. and 3 *slips inserted*.

### No. 804.

The History of the "**Philanthropic Lodge**," No. 304, Leeds, 1794-1894, by C. Letch Mason. Illustrated. (200 *numbered copies.*) *A handsome volume.* 4to. Leeds. 224 *pp*.

### No. 308.

An Historical Sketch of ["**Prince George Lodge**," No. 308,] Freemasonry at Bottoms, Eastwood, near Todmorden, Yorkshire, by John E. Craven. 8vo. Manchester, 1886. 96 *pp*.

> This Lodge is the "Prince George," although not so stated on the title page. Its warrant is dated 18th February, 1796

### No. 309.

Sketch History of the "**Lodge of Harmony**," No. 309, Fareham, Hants, by W. H. Barrell. 8vo. Fareham, 1909. 70 *pp*

### No. 312.

History of ["**Lion Lodge**," No. 312] Freemasonry in Whitby, from 1764 to 1897, by Rev. E. Fox Thomas, P.M. 8vo. Whitby, 1897. 70 *pp*. and 3 *plates*. (300 copies).

> An Appendix was issued afterwards as a separate pamphlet, viz.: "An Account of the Centenary Celebrations of the Lion Lodge, No. 312, Whitby, and the Meeting of the Provincial Lodge of North and East Yorks., held at Whitby, 15th July, 1897." 8vo. Whitby, 1898. *Plate and Pages numbered 73 to 111.*

### No. 320.

"**Lodge of Loyalty**," No. 320 (formerly Nos. 585, 603, 402). Mottram in Longdendale, Cheshire. Centenary Festival, October 26th, 1898. Post 4to. Ashton-under-Lyne. 50 *pp*.

### No. 328.

The History of "**St. John's Lodge**," No. 328 (formerly No. 616), Torquay, by John Chapman, P.M. 8vo. London and Torquay, 1894. 32 *pp*.

### No. 329.

Centenary History, 1810-1910, An Epitome of 100 Years Masonic Work of "**Lodge of Brotherly Love**," No. 329, Yeovil. Illustrated. 8vo. Yeovil, (1910).

Collation (viii) 243 *pp*.

> This work is the result of the united efforts of a committee of Messrs. Nosworthy, Raymond, Whitcomb, Buchanan, and Collins. The history contains lengthy notices of two notable London Coroners, "Dr. Danford Thomas" and "Dr. W. Wynn Westcott," Supreme Magus of the Rosicrucians of England, and Author of many well-known works on Mystic and Occult Sciences. The Lodge was consecrated at Martock, Somerset, as No. 617, on 19th April, 1810; it then became No. 624 (1832), No. 412 (1863), and now No. 329.

### No. 331.

Records of "**Phœnix Lodge of Honour and Prudence,**" No. 331, Truro, Cornwall, by John H. Ferris, P.M. 8vo. (1890). 4 *pp*.

### No. 336.

A Centenary Souvenir and Short History of "**Lodge Benevolence,**" No. 336, Marple, Stockport, 1809-1909, compiled by Ralph Andrews, P.M. 4to. N.P. or D. [1909.]
Collation (xxii), 75 *pp*., 11 plates.

### No. 340.

By-Laws of the "**Alfred Lodge,**" No. 340, Oxford, held at the Masonic Hall, with a History of the Lodge and a List of the Brethren from 1814 to 1884. 32mo. 1885. 64 *pp*.

### No. 357.

By-Laws of the "**Apollo University Lodge,**" No. 357, Oxford, with a History of the Lodge, by G. F. Lamert. 12mo. Oxford, 1869.

By-Laws of the "**Apollo University Lodge,**" No. 357, Oxford, to which is added a History of the Lodge, List of the Members, &c. 4th Edition. Edited by Bros. Pickard, Morrell, etc. 32mo. 1881. 174 *pp*. *Fifth Edition.* Edited by Rev. H. Adair Pickard 1888. 196 *pp*.

### No. 360.

A History of the "**Pomfret Lodge,**" No. 360, Northampton, by Thomas P. Dorman, P.M. Illustrated. 8vo. Northampton, 1910.
Collation (iv) 175 *pp*.

### No. 375.

History of the "**Lambton Lodge,**" No. 375, Chester-le-Street Durham, by Rt. Hon. Lord Barnard, D.C.L., with By-Laws, &c., 1824 to 1908. 16mo. N.P. 27 *pp*.

### No. 382.

Masonry in London and Middlesex, being the History of the old "**St. James's Lodge,**" (1740-1813) and the "**Royal Union Lodge,**" No. 382 (1825 to recent times), and comprising much information of Interest to Masons generally, by W. H. Reed, P.M. Illustrated. 8vo. London, 1906.
Collation (xxii) 248 *pp*.

### No. 387.

History of the "**Airedale Lodge**," No. 387, Shipley, giving also incidentally (by Notes of the foundation of each Lodge in Chronological order) a Record of the progress of Freemasonry in Yorkshire, by J. Ramsden Riley, P.M. 4to. 1877. *Second Edition*, 1878. *Third Edition*, 1880.
Collation of 3rd Edition (viii) 128 *pp*.

### No. 403.

History of the "**Hertford Lodge**," No. 403, from 1829-1879, by Thomas S. Carter. 12mo. Hertford, 1879. 72 *pp*.

### No. 416.

Bye-Laws for the regulation of the "**Surrey Lodge**" No. 416 (formerly No. 603) Reigate, with an Historical Sketch and list of officers, etc. 32mo. Redhill, 1882. 37 *pp*.

The History of the "**Surrey Lodge**," No. 416, (formerly No. 603) established at Reigate 1834; to which is prefixed a Sketch of Masonry, &c., compiled as a memorial of the 50th anniversary of the Lodge, by John Lees, P.M. *Illustrated*. 8vo. (1884).
Collation (vii) 84 *pp*.

### No. 418.

An Epitome of the History of the "**Menturia Lodge**," No. 418, Hanley, from 1834 to 1884, by E. V. Greatbatch, P.M. 8vo. Hanley, 1894. 22 *pp*.

### No. 425.

Antiquity of Chester Masonry, "**The Royal Chester and Cestrian Lodges**," by John Armstrong. Portraits. 8vo. Chester, 1900. 85 *pp*.
See also "Extinct Lodges," Chester.

### No. 445.

A History of the "**Lodge of Fidelity**," No. 652 (now No. 445) Towcester, Northamptonshire, by Thomas P. Dorman, P.M. 8vo. Northampton, 1909. 54 *pp. and* 1 *plate*.

### No. 448.

History of the "**Lodge of St. James**," No. 448, Halifax, from 1837-1890, with an account of the consecration of the Freemason's Hall, Halifax, by Austin Roberts, P.M. 4to. Leeds, 1895. 107 *pp*.

### No. 463.

The History of the "**East Surrey Lodge of Concord**," No. 463 (formerly No. 680) Croydon, with a Record of some of its leading events from its consecration in 1839 to January, 1890, &c., compiled from the Minute Books of the Lodge C. H. Woodward, P.M. 16mo. 1879. *Second edition*, 1890, 50 *pp*.

### No. 475.

A Short History of Freemasonry and of the Bedfordshire "**Lodge of St. John the Baptist**," No. 475, 1841-1891, by William Austin, P.M. 8vo. Luton, 1891.

Collation (iv) 124 *pp*.

### No. 478.

Bye-Laws for the Government of the "**Churchill Lodge**," No. 478, Oxford, with a History of the Lodge, edited by H. R. Cooper Smith, M.A. 32mo. (Oxford), 1877. 78 *pp*.

### No. 526.

A History of the "**Lodge of Honour**," No. 526 (late No. 769) Wolverhampton (principally condensed from the Minute Books) from 1846 to 1896, by Thos. J. Barnett, P.M., 1896, and an appendix, 1897. Portraits, &c. 8vo. *Privately circulated*.

Collation of History (x) 38 *pp*.

„ Appendix 18 *pp*.

### No. 533.

Records of the "**Eaton Lodge**," No. 533, Congleton, compiled by Captain Astley Terry, W.M. Illustrated. 8vo. Congleton, Cheshire, 1877.

Collation (xvi) 72 *pp*.

### No. 546.

Masonic Records (chiefly of the "**Etruscan Lodge**"), No. 546, Longton, Staffordshire. Compiled by W. R. Blair, P.M. 8vo. Longton, 1908.

Collation 119 *pp*.

Appendix (xvi) and 15 plates (one folding).

### No. 569.

A Little History of the "**Fitzroy Lodge**," (The Honourable Artillery Company) No. 569, London, by Henry F. Adlard. 8vo. London. October 30th, 1903.

<small>Collation (vii.) 37 (iii.) *pp.*, and Portrait.</small>

### No. 587.

History of the "**Howe Lodge**," No. 587 (formerly No. 857), Birmingham, 1851-1901, by A. D. Brooks, J.W. 8vo. (Birmingham), 1901. 35 *pp.*

### No. 602.

Fifty three years in the life of the "**North York Lodge**," No. 602. Middlesbrough, (1852-1905), by Alfred Sockett, W.M. Portraits. 8vo. Middlesbrough, 1905. 92 *pp.*

### No. 611.

Notes on the History of the "**Lodge of the Marches**," No. 611, Ludlow, and its predecessors, "The Mercian Lodge," Ludlow, and the "Silurian Lodge," Kingston, by T. J. Salway. Folio. Margate, 1892.

<small>This article appeared in the A. Q. C. Transactions, Vol. V., pp. 77-80. The Mercian Lodge became merged into the Silurian Lodge A.D. 1805, which was warranted A.D. 1791.</small>

### No. 636.

History of Lodge "**De Ogle**," No. 636, Morpeth, 1854-1904, by J. T. Proctor, P.M. 8vo. Newcastle-on-Tyne, 1906. 64 *pp. and 7 plates.*

### No. 707.

A History of **St. Mary's Lodge**," No. 707, Bridport, (1857-1907), together with some account of the rise and progress of Speculative Freemasonry in West Dorset, by A. M. Broadley, P.M., &c. 8vo. Bridport, 1907.

<small>Collation (xii) 80 *pp.* and 8 plates.</small>

### No. 731.

Fifty Years of the "**Arboretum Lodge**," [No. 731 Derby] 1858-1908, with brief references to Freemasonry in the Province of Derbyshire before 1858. Compiled by Joseph Bland, P.M. 4to. Derby, 1908. 31 *pp. and 3 plates. A handsome volume.*

### No. 739.

Notes on the Records of the "**Temperance Lodge**," No. 739, Birmingham (originally No. 1041), 1858-1908, by C. J. Fowler, P.M. 8vo. [Birmingham], April, 1903. 32 *pp*.

### No. 778.

The "**Bard of Avon Lodge**," No. 778, Hampton Court; a Record by J. C. Parkinson, W.M. *Privately circulated*. 4to. London, 1872. 196 *pp*.

> This Lodge was held at Stratford-on-Avon from 1859 to 1872, whence it was removed to the Province of Middlesex.

### No. 779.

History of the "**Lodge Ferrers and Ivanhoe**," No. 779, Ashby-de-la-Zouch, by John T. Thorp. Illustrated. 8vo. Leicester, 1909.

> This Lodge History, with several others now defunct, is contained in a larger work called "History of Freemasonry in Ashby-de-la-Zouch." 1809-1909. *Vide Article*.

### No. 792.

The History of Freemasonry in Grimsby from 1757 to 1892, by Anderson Bates, P.M., comprising "**The** "**Spurn and Humber**," "**The Apollo**," "**The Pelham Pillar**," No. 792, "**The St. Alban's**," and "**The Smyth**" Lodges. 8vo. Grimsby, 1892. 80 *pp. and Portrait*.

### No. 803.

History of "**St. Andrew's Lodge**," No. 803 (formerly No. 1105), Biggleswade, by J. B. Emmerson, P.M. 8vo. February, 1896. 17 *pp*.

### No. 804.

Bye-Laws and History of the "**Carnarvon Lodge**," No. 804, Havant, contained in "Freemasonry at Havant," &c., by a P.M., *i.e.* [Thomas Francis, P.M., &c.]. 16mo. 44 *pp*.

### No. 823.

A History of the "**Everton Lodge**," No. 823, Liverpool, 1860-1910. [Published by permission of the W. Deputy Provincial Grand Master and by Authority of the Lodge]. 8vo. Liverpool, 1911. 135 *pp*.

> This History was the work of a committee consisting of Bros. T. J. Carefull, J. J. Boyle. R. W. Gow. L. G. Davey, W. Griffiths, Past Masters, &c.

### No. 839.

The History of the "**Royal Gloucester Lodge**," No. 839, Gloucester (1785-1852), read 2nd January, 1885, by Thomas Taynton, P.M. 12mo. Gloucester, 1885. 16 *pp*.

### No. 869.

"**Gresham Lodge**," No. 869, Cheshunt Park, Herts, a Review of the past 21 years, with notes from the Minutes, by Walter E. Gompertz. P.M. 32mo. 1882. 26 *pp*.

The Manor of Andrewes and Le Motte, the present home of "**The Gresham Lodge**" of Freemasons, being an historical account of Cheshunt Great House from the 14th century, &c., by F. D. Rees Copestick. Plate. 4to. London, 1884. 30 *pp*.

### No 910.

Freemasonry in Pontefract from February, 1862, to February, 1902, being the history of the "**Lodge St. Oswald**," No. 910, Pontefract, for forty years, &c., by Edmund Lord, P.M. 8vo. Leeds, 1902.
Collation (iv) 148 *pp*. and 16 plates.

### No. 976.

A short History of the "**Royal Clarence Lodge**" No. 976 (formerly No. 695), Bruton, Somerset, from 1841 to the present time, compiled from the Minutes of the Lodge and other sources, by E. N. Hayter, P.M. 8vo. Yeovil, [1898]. 20 *pp*.

### No. 1010.

Annals of the "**Kingston Lodge**," No. 1010, Hull, 16mo. 1869. *Other editions appeared*, 1884, 1887 and 1890. 44 *pp*.
This History appears as part of the publication known as the "Hull Directory."

### No. 1040.

Record of the "**Sykes Lodge**." No. 1040, Driffield, Yorks., 1865 to 1905, compiled by Alex. T. Brand, W.M. 8vo. Driffield [1906]. 24 *pp*.

### No. 1101.

History of the "**Grey Friars Lodge**," No. 1101, Reading, by G. Thome Phillips, P.M. Illustrated. 8vo. Reading and Wellington College, Berks, 1910.
Collation (vi) 115 *pp*.

### No. 1167.

The Alnwick MS. and Records of the "**Alnwick Lodge**" No. 1167 (from 1703), by W. J. Hughan, P.M. Folio. London, 1871.

This is a reprint from the "Freemason," 1871.

The "**Alnwick Lodge**" Minutes, by W. H. Rylands. Folio. Margate, 1901.

This article appeared in the A.Q.C. Transactions, Vol. XIV., *pp.* 4-26.

### No. 1221.

Annals, with the Bye-Laws and Regulations of the "**Defence Lodge**," No. 1221, Leeds, by William Watson, P.M. 16mo. Leeds, 1879. 26 *pp.*

### No. 1357.

Chronicles of the "**Cope Lodge**," No. 1357, Sale, Cheshire, 1871-1892. 4to. Cloth. *Privately circulated.* 36 *pp.*

This Record was compiled by a Committee of "Bros. Simcock, Griffiths, and Langridge."

### No. 1416.

History of [The] "**Falcon Lodge**," No. 1416, Thirsk, from the consecration in 1872 to the Installation of the Worshipful Master in 1910, by Edwin Charlesworth. 8vo. [Thirsk, Yorkshire]. 78 *pp.*

### No. 1447.

Account of the present state of the "**St. Matthew's Lodge**," No. 488 [Now No. 1447], Barton-upon-Humber, Lincolnshire, Bye-Laws, &c. 8vo. Barton, 1819. 30 *pp.*

### No. 1514.

A short History of the "**Thornhill Lodge**," No. 1514, Lindley, Huddersfield, 1874-1895, compiled by W. A. Beevers, Secretary. 8vo. (Huddersfield, 1896). 11 *pp.*

### No. 1671.

Some notes from the History of the "**Mizpah Lodge**," No. 1671, London, February, 1876, to March, 1908, by Ralston Balch, W.M. 32mo. [London], 1908. *Unpaged.* (20 *pp.*)

### No. 1783.

"**Albert Edward Lodge**," No. 1783, Huddersfield, the History of its Minority, by Edwin Sykes, S.D. 8vo. Huddersfield, 1900. 23 *pp.*

### No. 1829.

Coming of Age; a retrospect of the "**Burrell Lodge**," No. 1829, Brighton, Sussex, by A. J. Carpenter, P.M. 8vo. (Brighton), 1900. 19 *pp*.

### No. 1874.

Notes on the History of the "**Lechmere Volunteer Lodge**," No. 1874, Balsall Heath, Kidderminster, February, 1881 to 1906, by Charlie D. Eaton, P.M. 4to. 28 *pp*.

### No. 2033.

A Short History of the "**University Lodge of London**," No. 2033, by W. J. Spratling. 20mo. London, 1884.

### No. 2069.

Records of a year's work of "**Lodge of Prudence**," No. 2069, Leeds, by C. Letch Mason. *Privately circulated.* 8vo. London, 1887. 24 *pp*.

### No. 2208.

"**Horsa Lodge**," No. 2208, Bournemouth. First Conversazione 23rd February, 1897, at the Masonic Hall, Bournemouth. 4to. 32 *pp*.

Contains a fine List of Exhibits of Jewels, Medals, Seals, &c.

### No. 2346.

"**Warrant Officer's Lodge**," No. 2346 [London]. Words and Music for use in the Ceremonies, compiled by W. F. Cheesman, P.M. and respectfully dedicated to the founders. 4to. [London]. 18th January, 1895.

### No. 2494.

Transactions of the "**Humber Installed Master's Lodge**," No. 2494, Hull, Yorkshire. Vols. I. to III. (now publishing). 8vo. Hull, 1894 to 1907.

    Collation Vol. I. *pp*. 1-94.
       „     Vol. II. *pp*. 95-265.
       „     Vol. III. (iv) *pp*. 266-397 and 24 plates.

### No. 3255.

An Account of the Formation, Consecration and First Year's Work of the "**Fairfax Lodge**," No. 3255, Guiseley, Yorks. *Printed for Private circulation.* 72 *pp*. and 14 *plates*.

The Historical Notes are by Bros. H. Speight and W. R. Makins.

# EXTINCT LODGES.

### Ashby-de-la-Zouch.

History of Freemasonry in Ashby-de-la-Zouch, 1809 to 1909, being an account of all the Masonic Bodies which have been established there during the past century, by John T. Thorp, P.M. *Illustrated.* 8vo. Leicester, 1909. 99 *pp*.

Contains a History of the Extinct "Ivanhoe Lodge," No. 631, 1836 to 1841.

### Chester.

The History of the "**Royal Lodge,**" of Freemasons, at Chester, as told by its Minutes, 1738 to 1767, by T. B. Whytehead, P.M. 8vo. 1884. 12 *pp*.

This is a Reprint from the "Freemason," 1884.

### Cumberland.

Some Notes on old Cumberland Lodges, by W. F. Lamonby, folio, Margate, 1895.

A.C.Q. Transactions Vol. vii. *pp*. 25-26.

### French Prisoners' Lodges.

A Brief Account of twenty-six Lodges and Chapters of Freemasons established and conducted by French Prisoners of War in England and elsewhere between 1756 to 1814, by John T. Thorp. 8vo. Leicester, 1900. 134 *pp*. and 18 *plates*.

### Gloucester.

The History of the "**Royal Gloucester Lodge,**" of Freemasons (1785 to 1852), read January 2nd, 1885 at the "Royal Gloucestershire Lodge," No. 839, by Thomas Taynton, P.M. 12mo. Gloucester [1885]. 16 *pp*.

### Hull.

A Glance at the Records of Two Extinct Hull Lodges ["**The Rodney Lodge,**" No. 436, founded 1781; and "**The Phœnix Lodge,**" No. 368] by G. L. Shackles, P.M. Folio, Margate, 1904.

A.Q.C. Transactions, Vol. xvii., *pp*. 181-200.

## Leicester.

Memorials of Lodge No 91 (Antients) Leicester, together with detailed List of Members, 1761 to 1821, compiled by John T. Thorp. 8vo. Leicester, 1898. 52 *pp.* and 5 *plates*.

> From this old Lodge bearing warrant dated 26th September, 1761, sprang the two present Leicester Lodges, viz., "**St. John's Lodge**," No. 299, and the "**Knights of Malta**," No. 50, Hinckley.

## Lincoln.

The old Lodge at Lincoln, by William Dixon. Folio. Margate, 1891. 14 *pp.*

> A.Q.C. Transactions, Vol. II., *pp.* 97-108.

## Norfolk.

The Lodge held at the "Maid's Head," Norwich, in 1724. Folio. Margate, 1902.

> A.Q.C. Transactions, Vol. XV., *pp.* 175-6.

The Great Lodge, Swaffham, Norfolk, 1764-1785, by Hamon le Strange, P.G.D.

> A.Q.C. Transactions, Vol. XX., *pp.* 232-248.

## Sussex.

Minutes of an Extinct Lodge ["**The Royal Sussex Lodge**," No. 720, Worthing, erased 5th September, 1838], by E. A. T. Breed, P.M. Folio. Margate, 1904.

> A.Q.C. Transactions, Vol. XVII., *pp.* 37-55.

## Taunton.

Bye-Laws of the "**Lodge Liberty and Sincerity**," No. 382, Taunton, (with Minutes, September, 1817 to April, 1882, in M.SS.). 4to. Taunton, 1817.

> This unique copy is preserved in the Grand Lodge Library, London

## York.

History of the "**Apollo Lodge**," York, &c. (1705 to 1805), by W. J. Hughan, with Appendices. Illustrated. 8vo. London, 1889. 128 *pp.*

# PROVINCIAL GRAND LODGES
## AND
# COUNTY HISTORIES.

### Berkshire.

Sketch of Freemasonry in Berkshire, 1725 to 1891, by J. T. Morland, D.P.G.M.; this is contained in "The Register" for 1892. 8vo. Newbury.

### Bristol.

Freemasonry in Bristol, compiled from John Lane's "Masonic Records" and other sources, by John Gard, P.M. 8vo. 1889. 8 *pp*. *Privately circulated.*
  Contains a list of extinct and existing Bristol Lodges.

A History of Freemasonry in Bristol, by Arthur C. Powell and Joseph Littleton. 8vo. Illustrated. Bristol, 1910. *A handsome and voluminous work.*
  Collation (xii) 926 *pp*.

### Berks and Bucks.

History of the Provincial Grand Lodge of Berkshire and Buckinghamshire, with By-Laws, by William Biggs, P.M. 8vo. Reading, 1871. 36 *pp*.
  The "Etonian Lodge of St. John," Windsor, has the enviable distinction of holding the oldest existing "Atholl" warrant (A.D. 1794).

### Buxton and Longnor.

History of Freemasonry in Buxton and Longnor, by Sydney Taylor. 4to. Buxton, 1906.

### Cheshire.

A History of Freemasonry in Cheshire, being a Record of all extinct and existing Lodges, &c., by John Armstrong. 8vo. London, 1901. (500 *numbered copies*).
  Collation (xxii) 540 *pp*. and 9 *plates*.

### Cornwall.

Some account of the Provincial Grand Lodge of Cornwall, etc. 8vo. Truro, 1865. 40 *pp.* and 2 *tables.*

### Cornwall (West).

History of Freemasonry in West Cornwall, from 1765 to 1828, with Chapters on the Mark, R. A., and K. T. Ceremonies, by Joseph G. Osborn, P.M., etc. 8vo. Penzance, 1901.
Collation (viii) 246 *pp*.

### Cumberland and Westmoreland.

History of Craft Masonry in Cumberland and Westmoreland from 1740 to the present day; edited by W. F. Lamonby, P.M. 8vo. Carlisle, 1879.
Collation (xii) 128 *pp*. and *plate.*

### Devon and Cornwall.

Freemasonry in Devon and Cornwall from 1732-1889, by W. J. Hughan, P.G.D. 8vo. London, 1889. 128 *pp*.
This work forms the Introduction (10 *pp*.) to a work Edited by J. Chapman called "*Masonic Orations.*"

### Devonshire.

A short account of the Provincial Grand Lodge, with By-Laws. 8vo. 1843. 32 *pp*. *Other editions*, 1847, 80 *pp*. 1876, 50 *pp*.

### Durham.

Freemasonry in the Province of Durham, Sunderland, [by Sir Cuthbert Sharp, D. Prov., G.M.?] 8vo. Durham, 1836.
Collation (viii) 26 *pp*.

### Exeter.

The Master's Lodge at Exeter, by W. J. Hughan. Folio. Margate, 1894.
A.C.Q. Transactions, vol. VII., *pp*. 63-71.

### Hampshire.

Freemasonry at Havant; a Page in the History of Freemasonry in Hampshire, by Thomas Francis, P.M. 12mo. Portsmouth, 1892. 45 *pp*.

### Hertfordshire.

History of Freemasonry in Hertfordshire, by G. Blizzard Abbott. 8vo. London, 1893. 467 *pp*.

### Kent.

A Brief Sketch of Freemasonry in Canterbury, from 1730 to 1880; with an account of Ceremonies and Addresses at the Laying of the Foundation Stone of the Masonic Temple in that City. 16mo. Canterbury, 1880. 36 *pp*.

This is a reprint from the "Canterbury Press," March 6th, 1880, and contains a brief History of Lodge No. 31, with some others.

### Leicester and Rutland.

A History of the Provincial Grand Lodge of Leicestershire, &c., including Notices of Private Lodges and Chapters in the Province, &c., by William Kelly, P.G.M. 8vo. Leicester, 1870. 112 *pp*.

### Lincolnshire.

A History of the Provincial Grand Lodge of Lincolnshire from 1792-1867, by C. E. Lucas, Prov. G.S. 8vo. Louth, 1867. 26 *pp*. and *tables*.

A History of Freemasonry in Lincolnshire, being a record of all extinct and existing Lodges, Chapters, &c.; a Century of the Working of Provincial Grand Lodge, and "**The Witham Lodge**," with Biographical Notices, &c., by William Dixon, P.M. 297. 8vo. Lincoln, 1894. 365 *pp*.

### Norfolk.

A History of Freemasonry in Norfolk, 1724 to 1895, by Hamon Le Strange, P.G.D., England. 8vo. Norwich, 1896.

Collation (xvi) 401 *pp*. and 1 *plate*.

### Northumberland.

Northumbrian Masonry and the development of the Craft in England, by John Strachan, Q.C., Grand Registrar of England, &c. *Fine plates*. 8vo. London, 1898. 220 *pp*.

### Oxfordshire.

A History of Freemasonry in Oxfordshire, by E. L. Hoskins W.M. 32mo. Oxford, 1882.

Collation (viii) 58 *pp*.

### Shropshire.

History of Freemasonry in the Province of Shropshire, etc., by Alexander Graham. 8vo. Shrewsbury, 1892.
Collation (xv) 232 *pp*.

### Staffordshire.

An attempt at compiling a History of Freemasonry in Stafford, to which is prefixed a short Sketch of the History of Masonry in England from the earliest times, by T. Ward Chalmers, P.M. 12mo. Stafford, 1882.
Collation (viii) 84 *pp*.

A History of Freemasonry in the Province of Staffordshire, by Frederic W. Willmore, P.M. Folio. Wolverhampton and London, 1905. 174 *pp*. and 2 *plates*.

A fatality seems to have attended the authorship of this Work; it was commenced by a Bro. Willmore who unfortunately died in 1902; it was then continued by Bro. Dunbar Steen, who also died in 1905, and the work of completion fell into the hands of Colonel Walter Walker, who brought it to a successful termination.

### Sussex.

History of Freemasonry in Sussex, containing a Sketch of the Lodges Past and Present, with numerical Tables of Extinct and Existing Lodges, &c., by Thomas Francis, W.M. *Coloured plates*. 8vo. London, 1883. 150 *pp*.

### Wiltshire.

A History of Freemasonry in Wiltshire, including an account of the Provincial Grand Lodge and its subordinate Lodges, &c., by Frederick H. Goldney, P.G.D. 4to. N.P. 1880. *For presentation only.*
Collation (viii) 200 *pp*.

Notes on Freemasonry in the Town of Marlborough, 1768-1834, compiled from various sources by J. E. S. Tuckett, P.M. 8vo. Marlborough, 1910. (*Privately circulated*).
Collation (iv) 42 *pp*.

Contains Histories of several defunct Lodges, viz., "The Castle Inn," No. 249; "Wilts Militia," No. 282, afterwards "Lodge of Loyalty," No. 356 and 249, which is now revived under the same name and No. 1533. The work exhibits considerable research, and is a valuable contribution to our collection.

### Worcestershire.

A History of the Provincial Grand Lodge of Worcestershire, compiled from official sources by Albert Brown, P.M., with By-Laws. 8vo. N.P. 1881. 102 *pp*.

## Yorkshire.

A Short History of the Provincial Grand Lodge of the North and East Ridings of Yorkshire, &c., by Dr. John P. Bell, D. Prov. G.M. 8vo. Kingston-upon-Hull, 1868. 48 *pp*.

"Masonic Sketches and Reprints." (1) History of Freemasonry in York. (2) Unpublished Records of the Craft, by W. J. Hughan, P.M. 8vo. London, 1871.
 Collation Part I., 112 *pp*.; Part II., 54 *pp*.
 *The First Part was also printed in the "Kingston Masonic Annual," 1871.*

(1) Freemasonry in York, 1878. 8vo. 12 *pp*. (2) Freemasonry in XVIII. Century, as told by an old Newspaper file, 1884. 8vo. 14 *pp*. (3) Some Ancient York Masons and their Early Haunts. 8vo. 14 *pp*. 1884.
 All by T. B. Whytehead.

The Grand Lodge at York, by T. B. Whytehead. Folio. Margate, 1889  7 *pp*.
 A.Q.C Transactions, Vol. II., *pp* 110-115.

The York Grand Lodge, by W. J. Hughan; and the Relicts of the Grand Lodge at York, by T. B. Whytehead. Folio. Margate, 1900. 55 *pp*. and 11 *plates*.
 A.Q.C. Transactions, Vol XIII, *pp* 4 & 93.

The York Grand Lodge; a Brief Sketch, by W. J. Hughan. 8vo. London (*not for reproduction*), 1900. 16 *pp*.
 A Reprint from "*The Freemason,*" January, 1900.

"The Yorkshire Lodges,"; a Century of Yorkshire Freemasonry, by J. Ramsden Riley. Illustrated. 4to. London, 1885. 120 *pp*. *Supplement* of 4 *pp*. "Notes on Yorkshire Lodges" appeared in the Edition of 1887.

# FINIS.